A Devotional for Understanding and Acceptance

Volume 1

A Devotional Series

by

Dr. Jay B Newman

About The Author

Jay Newman is a founding partner of Culture by Choice™, a company that focuses on helping clients create the culture they desire by determining what exists now, who the people are that make up that existing culture, and then creating the coaching processes needed to move the company from where they are to where they want to be. Jay received his Doctorate in Education Leadership from Vanderbilt University in 1984. Jay spent over 35 years in public education teaching Biology and Chemistry and then moving into the administrative ranks. When he retired from education in 2006, he left having served his final 8 years as the County Superintendent of Schools in St. Joseph County Michigan. He returned to the superintendency in 2013-14 for a one-year interim position with the Colon Community Schools in Michigan.

Jay and his wife Barb attended Augustana College in Rock Island, Illinois. While at Augustana, Jay had several professors that had a lasting impact on his thinking and faith. Some of these were teachers of Religion, while others were coaches and teachers in Science, Math, and History. Jay had several friends who attended the seminary after college, while Jay went into public education. Jay's faith was critical in his decision-making and career trajectory.

Teaching Biology and Chemistry and later going into the administrative ranks, Jay stayed true to his Christian Faith. He challenged the status quo in education and looked for answers beyond traditional school textbooks. Believing that the best knowledge is knowledge that can withstand critical arguments, he was always open to discussing a variety of topics. Among these were evolution, quantum Physics, Environmental Sciences, and leadership.

Jay and Barb have been active members of the United Methodist Church for over 50 years and even though there has been a great deal of controversy in the church over the past decade or two, they do not see these issuers as impinging upon their faith. All of the controversy should be left to God, and we Christians should just fulfill Christ's two great commandments: Love God with all your being and love your fellow human beings as Jesus loved us.

A synopsis of this Series

Book series # 1is titled **<u>A Devotional for Understanding and Acceptance</u>**. In the works is a second series that will be titled **<u>A Devotional for the Love of God</u>**. I have not yet pondered the third in this series of books. Each series will be four books, with each book comprising the Daily Devotionals I have written for each year. Series # 1 was completed during 2023 and Series # 2 is planned for 2024. Volume 1 for Series # 1 covers January 1 through the end of March 2023. I hope you enjoy this series and even more, I hope you find inspiration to live a life filled with the Love of Christ.

Some of the topics might seem to be controversial for some people, but my intention is always to share my sense of God's Love as it has been shared with me. Paramount in my intentions is the simple fact that as Christians we already know that we cannot earn our way to heaven. If we could earn our way to heaven, there would have been no need for Christ to come to Earth and be sacrificed for our salvation. With that in mind, it should also be acknowledged that, if we cannot earn our way to heaven, we cannot facilitate the entrance into heaven for any other person by any means than simply sharing God's Love and encouraging them to accept Christ as their savior while, in turn, sharing God's Love with all they encounter as well.

Should you find this book and others in the series to be useful in your faith journey, feel free to contact me and let me know. How we discover Christ and invite him into our lives is not as important as the simple act of doing so. I encourage all people everywhere to really investigate the promise of Jesus and the peace and love he will bring into your life when you simply turn your life over to him. Grace, Peace, and Love to all! AMEN!

Table of Contents

An Introduction to this Devotional Series

Introductory Comments: I made a commitment, at the beginning of 2023, to write a devotional and post it for my colleagues, friends, and acquaintances. I have nearly completed that task. As I write these introductory remarks for this first installment of these devotionals to be published, it is December 14, 2023, and I have not missed a single day of posting these. The response has been remarkable. I have been constantly encouraged to continue to write them and now to publish them for everyone to enjoy and receive inspiration from. Many of the readers have told me how inspirational they have found my words, but I must confess, these are not my words, but my utterings of what God has revealed through the scriptures, the words of those people I talk to and interact with on a daily basis and the thoughts that the Holy Spirit has put into my brain.

If it were not for the comments and encouraging words of so many faithful readers, (now more than 2,000 different people sending me positive feedback, challenging my assumptions, and urging me on) this project would have ended a long time ago. So I go forward with publishing the devotionals from 2023 and ready myself to continue writing through 2024 and as far into the future as God Continues to inspire my words and gives me the strength to put them down on a page. I have truly been blessed and I am eternally grateful for all those blessings. At the top of my blessing list is my Wife Barb, who has been so patient as I have often been writing early in the morning or late at night as I have been inspired to do.

My prayer for our world is that we will finally find Peace, Love, and Understanding! As a Baby Boomer Generation Member who has been blessed beyond what I deserve, I encourage every human to follow Christ's two Great Commandments: Love God with all your Being (Heart, Mind, Psyche, Body, and Spirit) and Love One another as He has loved us. No Greater Love has anyone than that they have given their life to save the life of others. Every aspect of my devotionals will be dedicated to Loving God who sacrificed His amazing son for our Salvation. This is a Labor of Love that focuses on Bring Love to our entire World! AMEN

Day 1

A Devotional for Understanding and Acceptance

Therefore, if anyone is in Christ, he is a new creation; the old has gone, the new has come! —

2 Corinthians 5:17

What does this statement by Paul really mean? This is not a concept to be trifled with. The Apostle Paul is telling us that Christ wants us to let our old ways die, bury them, and then experience a truly Christ-like rebirth! To be born again does not mean WE are required to do anything for ourselves. In fact, we are incapable of saving ourselves. The only thing we must do is acknowledge that through God's amazing LOVING GRACE, we have been redeemed.

Be thankful for the gift and remember, you earned nothing. So, stop trying to tell anyone else how to live. Jesus came to us because the religious leaders of the day were morally off the mark. Today, we seem to have found our way right back to that "bad place!" And I'm not talking about political leaders. I'm referring to all the "So-Called Christians" that would be swarming around a person accused of sexual bad behavior, (while ignoring starving children) ready to be part of the execution team. Remember, Christ

Challenged the crowd that was ready to kill by stoning, the woman. He asked them "who among you is without sin, let that person cast the first stone!" One-by one the crowd dispersed. Then Christ turns to the woman and says, "Where are your accusers now? No one remains to accuse you, nor will I! Go now, remember what happened here today, and therefore change your life. (Sin no more: might be easier than "CHANGE YOUR LIFE!" But God is asking to truly CHANGE!) When St. Paul states "Therefore, if anyone is in Christ, (s)he is a new creation:" he is telling us exactly what Christ wants us to do!

Our Prayer for today:

Heavenly Gracious God, we ask you to be with us in our journey. Left to our devices we may wander aimlessly, take too many wrong turns, and put words in your mouth that are completely opposite of what your intentions might have been. Let us not be so quick to condemn and be constantly reminded that out Lord and Savior, Jesus Christ forgave sins of many who elders of the day would have executed those people for. You are our Redeemer God, please help us act like it! AMEN

If you appreciate this first day of my Day-by-Day 365 Devotionals, let me know. Feel free to share them, they will never cost you a penny. If you would like to have a speaker, come to your community, just ask. We'll work with you to schedule a visit.

Day 2

A Devotional for Understanding and Acceptance

January 2, 2023

In the beginning there was nothing and into that nothing and out of nothing, SOMETHING WAS CREATED! "In the beginning was the word and the Word was with God and the Word was God. She was with God in the beginning." John 1:1 Does that sound crazy? Based on our concept of nothing, yes that's crazy! Based on Quantum Mechanics, it all makes sense. Even though Dr. Albert Einstein was not sure about "God," he very definitely knew that there were forces, powers, and energies about which we had and still have very much to learn!

Once the focus turned from the fundamental building blocks of matter being immutable; matter could neither be created or destroyed, to how does our understanding of relativity explain how our universe came into existence, the connection between science and religion started to emerge. As is usually the response to any threat of change in how we explain our human presence on this planet, many people have been very hesitant to embrace a different explanation. This is true for both those who deny the existence of God and those who are literalists in regard to the creation story as they understand it, from a more organized religion's point of view. While the most extreme points of view argued over faith versus godless evolution, most scientist spent their time trying to gain a better comprehension of how matter could be created through altering energy in a manner that converted wavelengths into particles and in so doing began to see that what we thought about God was viewed from a very human point of view! However, if we looked from the Quantum Field, it all made sense.

What do I really believe? I believe every life is sacred and the real "original sin," was the first time one of God's created creatures decided it knew better how to go about living than did the creator. With that incredible act of arrogance, we started our journey away from where the creator truly wanted us to be!

John 2:2-3 "He was God in the Beginning." "Through him (Our Savior Jesus) All things were made; without him nothing was made that has been made. In him was life and that life was light of men. The light shines in the darkness, the darkness has not understood it."

Our Prayer for today:

Holy Lord God, we pray that you will help us understand the glory and graciousness of your creation. We think we know, but too often fail to take into consideration the simple fact that our minds cannot conceive of all that is possible to You! Help us stop putting limitations on your capabilities and incredible power. The more we examine the mysteries of science, the more we understand the incredible simplicity it has in your realm. Keep us in your arms and teach us that there is nothing that Love cannot fix. Give us our daily requirements and keep us in your constant care. For you are omnipotent, omniscient, and omnipresent in our lives, and you are our hope and our salvation. AMEN

Day 3

A Devotional for Understanding and Acceptance

"Do not judge, and you will not be judged. Do not condemn, and you will not be condemned. Forgive, and you will be forgiven." Luke 6:37

I don't know about you, but I have definitely had judgement issues throughout my adult life. We've been trained to do so! Over the eons of time, we have worried about where our enemies are. Whether they be human, beast, supernatural, from beyond the planet, or from under the surface of the water or ground; It has never been in our own best interest to look at our continued success, through the lens of fear. Yet, we certainly are aware of a great number of people who continue to make their futures must less rewarding because of their excessive and powerful desire to keep to what they are familiar with and therefore will only include people that look like them, think like them, and believe what they believe. Jesus was fully aware that failure to explore novel ideas, unusual places, and unconventional solutions to recurring problems could be the undoing of humanity.

Will we continue to be so narrow-minded and self-protective that we miss the very real warning signs of the very real and pending apocalypse. It won't be Satan that brings us down. Satan can sit back, watch, and enjoy the show as we fight each other on our way to oblivion. What too many of us just don't realize is that both our Creator God and the Destroyer Satan have access to our HEARTS! Satan can move in the second our predominant emotions are hate, anger, jealousy, exclusivity, and/or the fear of the different, unknown, and change. You cannot love God and Hate what the Creator Created! When these extreme and harmful emotions become our guiding force, we lock Jesus outside. Remember Our Amazing, Loving Creator God sent Jesus to us to try to convince all of us of our need to change.

The Creator knows that we can be (every single, solitary human) very easily fooled into believing that we should carefully guard the very wrong thoughts and (amazingly 2,000+ years later) so many of us continue to think that these notions are very important and what we all, not only need to do but more importantly, this the only way to please God. Remember the 2 most important commandment are:

1. Love God

2. Love your Neighbor: and in Jesus' eyes you know who he thinks your neighbor is!

"As you have done to the least of these, so have you done to me!" Matthew: 25:40

Our Prayer for today:

Lord Jesus, we pray that you will teach us to Love as You have Loved. We make excuses as for why we cannot love certain people, but in your eyes; none of these excuses hold any sway. To Love Our Neighbor, and your definition of our neighbor, not ours, is an inclusive command. We cannot be exclusive and meet your expectations. Help us stop judging, so that we can enter your kingdom with the same measuring stick we have applied to others. These things we pray in <u>your Holy Name: AMEN</u>

Day 4

A Devotional for Understanding and Acceptance

In Matthew 9:27-31, we read: "As Jesus went on from there, two blind men followed him, calling out, 'Have mercy on us, Son of David!' When he had gone indoors, the blind men came to him, and he asked them, 'Do you believe that I am able to do this?' 'Yes, Lord, 'they replied. Then he touched their eyes and said, 'According to your faith let it be done to you' and their sight was restored. Jesus warned them sternly, 'See that no one knows about this.' But they went out and spread the news about him all over that region."

Now we've all heard about the miracles of Jesus, but did you pay very close attention to how this miracle happened? According to your faith let it be done to you' and their sight was restored. This is an important idea! You must have complete faith if you desire complete healing! If you have complete faith in God's healing power, as soon as you ask for healing, you know you have already been healed. God will take the ongoing steps for your healing. Don't question The Creator God's intention, capacity, love, and desire for you to be healed; completely!

How will this "healing" take place? God will use every tool he has made available to humankind! Doctors, healers, prayer circles, natural foods, and all other possible means. I saw a post on a social media site, that showed Linus from the Peanuts Comic Strip. In that piece, Linus makes this statement: "Trust the science is the most anti science statement ever made. Questioning science is how you do science!" Not really, trusting science is what has created some of the most amazing advancements in our human existence. What the real truth is, Scientists trust the science only when it has been verified through repeated positive experimental results and then only until a viable and better alternative is discovered. This cartoon defies that principle and quite often, those who adhere to what Linus is saying here, are succumbing to the errors too many non-scientists make; they cling to old science or inadequately tested science in order to keep real advancements from shaking up their comfortable worlds.

Consider this, Jesus tells us: "In my father's house, there are many rooms, if it were not so, I would tell you!" John 14:2. Yet too many of us want to limit access to his father's house! Why, because too many are afraid there just won't be enough room for me if we just let anyone in. That scarcity thinking results from believing that Our Creator God would create a world that would possibly be fraught with inadequate space to handle all of God's creation. This will cause us to hang on to ways of life that say: "Why should I care about 'THEM?' They are not my concern." However, Jesus says, "As you treat the least of these, so have you treated me!"

Our Prayer for today:

Gracious Creator God: Teach us to accept ALL and reject none. For in this inclusivity, we find redemption. By not excluding or condemning, we open the doors to redemption. It is not ours to say that this person here, or that person there is unworthy of Christ's Redemptive Love. Christ invites everyone to the table, and it is up to each to accept or reject the invitation. And there is no time limit on acceptance. The parable of the Vineyard workers is an excellent example of this concept. Those that come at the very end of the workday receive the same salvation as those who came earliest in the day. Indeed, we should all rejoice that another has found the promise! AMEN "trust the science" is the most anti science statement ever. Questioning science is how you do science!

Day 5

A Devotional for Understanding and Acceptance

Then Moses said to God, "Suppose I go to the People of Israel, and I tell them, 'The God of your fathers sent me to you'; and they ask me, 'What is his name?' What do I tell them?" Then God said to Moses, "I am that I am. Tell the people of Israel that I-am sent me!" Exodus 3:13

Can we talk for a moment about the names we give God? Do we need anything other than this! (I am) If we need another name, we just don't get it. What does it mean when we God says, in answer to the question "Who are you?" I AM-(That) I AM! What God wants us to know and fully comprehend is that whatever we need, HE IS ALL WE WILL EVER NEED! Is there anyone who is willing to advise us on what will cure any specific disease? How about a the Great I am! Yes, God says I AM ready, willing, and able to solve any problem you have!

So how can we connect with this incredible energy and will to be the answer to every possible problem we face. The concept is atonement: read the AT-ONE-MENT! When we pray and meditate on our relationship with GOD, what we must realize is that we cannot help ourselves by trying to bargain and negotiate with GOD!

However, when you quiet your mind and engage your essential spirit (soul) with the creative source (Holy Spirit) of God, and then know that The Holy Spirit wants to be At-One with your Soul, you begin to understand how AT-ONE-MENT, releasing your worldly desires and truly connecting with the Source of all life, is the greatest, most awesome solution producing process EVER.

"Whoever exalts himself will be humbled, and whoever humbles himself will be exalted." Matthew: 23;12

"For even the Son of Man came not to be served but to serve, and to give his life as a ransom for many." Mark: 10;45

We cannot achieve a true connection with God if we think we are so important that HE just must protect me! In order to connect, we must lose our pride, desire, sense of personal importance and worth and only want to do things that I AM, tells us are worthy, will make GOD proud, and fulfill God's desires for us.

My prayer for this Devotional:

Thank you, Creator of all that is, was, and ever will be! I am So incredibly thankful that The Great I AM, finds me worthy of even continuing my existence. My prayer is for a true, sincere, and honest connection to the source of all that creates the essence of our humanity. Let me find my one-ness with the Holy Spirit. AMEN

Day 6

A Devotional for Understanding and Acceptance

Who is worthy of salvation?

"When one of the Pharisees invited Jesus to have dinner with him, he went to the Pharisee's house and reclined at the table. A woman in that town who lived a sinful life learned that Jesus was eating at the Pharisee's house, so she came there with an alabaster jar of perfume. As she stood behind him at his feet weeping, she began to wet his feet with her tears. Then she wiped them with her hair, kissed them and poured perfume on them. When the Pharisee who had invited him saw this, he said to himself, 'If this man were a prophet, he would know who is touching him and what kind of woman she is—that she is a sinner.' "Jesus answered him, 'Simon, I have something to tell you.'

"'Tell me, teacher,' he said." "Two people owed money to a certain moneylender. One owed him five hundred denarii, and the other fifty. Neither of them had the money to pay him back, so he forgave the debts of both. Now which of them will love him more?" Simon replied, "I suppose the one who had the bigger debt forgiven."

"You have judged correctly," Jesus said. "Then he turned toward the woman and said to Simon, 'Do you see this woman? I came into your house. You did not give me any water for my feet, but she wet my feet with her tears and wiped them with her hair. You did not give me a kiss, but this woman, from the time I entered, has not stopped kissing my feet. You did not put oil on my head, but she poured perfume on my feet. Therefore, I tell you, her many sins have been forgiven—as her great love has shown. But whoever has been forgiven little loves little.' "Then Jesus said to her, "Your sins are forgiven." The other guests began to say among themselves, "Who is this who even forgives sins? Jesus said to the woman, "Your faith has saved you; go in peace."

Please take the time and make the effort to be more like Jesus. It isn't easy at first. We've been raised by well-meaning parents, teachers, preachers, political leaders, and "GOD" knows how many others, to be critical of those who are different and don't adhere to the same rules and beliefs we find comforting. Additionally, it is way too easy to ridicule those we see as unworthy and to shun those who don't measure up. If there ever was a human being who had the right to be picky, it was Jesus! But HE accepted all! All anyone needed was simply to believe and have faith that they would be forgiven AND IT WIL BE Done. We're told that we need to approach our faith as children do. According to Matthew 18, Jesus tells us "Whoever takes the lowly position of this child is the greatest in the kingdom of heaven."

Omniscient, omnipotent, omnipresent Lord of all, then for the Forgiveness I have found in your heart! I am so great full the price of my ransom from my prison of my own making has been paid in full. Amen.

Day 7

A Devotional for Understanding and Acceptance

What is C.H.E.E.L?

<u>Calm:</u> "Come to Me, all who are weary and heavy-laden, and I will give you rest. "Take My yoke upon you, and learn from Me, for I am gentle and humble in heart; and YOU SHALL FIND REST FOR YOUR SOULS. "For My yoke is easy, and My load is light." Matt 11:28-30

<u>Happy:</u> Blessed are the pure in heart, for they will see God. Matthew 5:8 What could possibly be a greater source of happiness than knowing your blessings can stem from a Pureness of heart? And how do we attain a pure heart; it is quite simple! Those who love all of God's Creation simply because God created it, fully understand. When we drive HATE AND ANGER OUT and replace all vestiges of those foul, self destructive emotions with those creative, compassionate emotions of Love, Hope, Charity, and kindness, we have begun our transformation into a new person.

<u>Empathetic:</u> "I feel compassion for the people because they have remained with Me now three days and have nothing to eat!

Mark 8:2. "Therefore, the kingdom of heaven is like a king who wanted to settle accounts with his servants.

As he began the settlement, a man who owed him ten thousand bags of gold was brought to him. Since he was not able to pay, the master ordered that he and his wife and his children and all that he had be sold to repay the debt.

At this the servant fell on his knees before him. 'Be patient with me,' he begged, 'and I will pay back everything.' The servant's master took pity on him, canceled the debt and let him go. Matthew 18:18-27 If I walk in my friends shoes, I will see what my friends overlook in me yet still call me friend. If I walk in my enemies shoes, I may find out where my flaws are and discover what makes me a danger in their eyes.

<u>Energetic:</u> This is the message we have heard from Him and announce to you, that God is Light, and in Him there is no darkness at all. 1John 1:5 What is Light? Visible light is a specific segment of the electromagnetic spectrum between 400 and 750 nm (a wavelength of light energy from 400 to 750 nanometers. A millimeter (mm) equals 1 million nanometers and an inch is equal to 25 mm. So, let us just say, the length of visible light waves, is really, really, really small! Let there be light! Let there be sound! Someone with excellent hearing can hear very high pitched sounds where the wavelength is 17 mm long and very low pitched sounds with wave lengths of over 15 meters. Sound and light are two different forms of energy. We use light therapy and sound therapy in medicine to help heal a variety of different maladies.

Love: And now these three remain: faith, hope and love. But the greatest of these is love. 1 Corinthians 13:13 And what is LOVE! Love is the source of all that is Good and Holy! LOVE is the Source of Life! God is LOVE, complete compassionate, and UNCONDITIONAL LOVE.

THE truest expression of LOVE can only come from those who recognize that without the heart of our LOVING GRACIOUS GOD, we will never truly be able to love; all else is love with conditions attached! When we say I'll love you if? You've missed the mark.

Let us offer up the prayer of St. Francis as our prayer to God and make that the guiding mantra of your Life!

Lord, make me an instrument of your peace: where there is hatred, let me sow love;

Where there is injury, pardon; where there is doubt, faith; where there is despair, hope; where there is darkness, light; where there is sadness, joy.

O divine Master, grant that I may not so much seek to be consoled as to console to be understood as to understand, to be loved as to love.

For it is in giving that we receive, it is in pardoning that we are pardoned, and it is in dying that we are born to eternal life.

Amen

Day 8

A Devotional for Understanding and Acceptance

How should we PRAY?

I desire therefore that the People pray everywhere, lifting up holy hands, without wrath and doubting. 1 Timothy 2:8

To some who were confident of their own righteousness and looked down on everyone else, Jesus told this parable:

Two men went up to the temple to pray, one a Pharisee and the other a tax collector. The Pharisee stood by himself and prayed: 'God, I thank you that I am not like other people—robbers, evildoers, adulterers—or even like this tax collector. I fast twice a week and give a tenth of all I get.' But the tax collector stood at a distance. He would not even look up to heaven, but beat his breast and said, 'God, have mercy on me, a sinner.' I tell you that this man, rather than the other, went home justified before God. For all those who exalt themselves will be humbled, and those who humble themselves will be exalted." Luke 18:9-14

Jesus had a level of tolerance and compassion that was boundless for those who were truly humble and wanted forgiveness. But, for those who wanted everyone to acknowledge how good, important, and religious they were, Jesus would let them know he was disappointed. Jesus would implore these "I'm better than those miserable sinners" people to change and if they would repent, Jesus would welcome them with open arms.

What are your prayers like? Do you pray with the heart of the tax collector? Or are your prayers like those of the Pharisee? My prayer is that you will become a gardener of peace, love and joy! To harvest these, you must plant the seeds, nourish them, water them and then just watch them grow! Amen

Day 9

A Devotional for Understanding and Acceptance

How do I know I AM SAVED?

Throughout my life I have failed many people. The living human being who has had to deal with my continuous shortcomings the most, is my wife. She has forgiven my transgressions and forgotten most of them, most of the time. However, from time to time, I'll pull some boneheaded move and some of those errors will come flooding back into her mind!

I am so fortunate to have been blessed by a force for good that only looks for the good in me and is willing to ignore all I've done that might derail my best intentions. The Creator God has my back. If I am willing to be changed from my old "needy, abhorrent, selfish past" being, into a new "best for the world" being, I know my God will allow me to enjoy the fruits of HIS labor. If I will just give up the struggles created by the old me and Allow God to me into becoming the brand new me, Jesus wants and begged all of us to become, not for his sake or even His Father's sake, but so that I may be welcomed into his eternal home, I know I am saved!

How do I know all of this? Jesus lays our path out for us in such a clear way, that there can be no mistaking who is eligible for Salvation. Everyone is eligible, no one is excluded. So, what is required for anyone to receive this amazing gift? Nothing, simply follow these two laws which Jesus said gave purpose and meaning to all of the laws and prophesies of the past; Love God (as Jesus loves God-with all his Heart, Mind, Body, and Soul) and Love Each other, in that same way! When we love God and each other, in this way, you will recognize the good in every other human being.

What would our World be like if WE, (the eternal and total WE) every single one of WE, truly followed Jesus' admonition for WE? You may say that I'm a dreamer; But I'm not the only ONE! Jesus hopes someday YOU'LL Join us, and the World will Live as ONE! Ah, the Ultimate Universal Atonement. When John Lennon, was murdered and his Soul (Spirit) was confronted by the Spirit of the living God, personified in Jesus; based on the meeting of these 2 loving hearts, what do you suppose happened? Truthfully, it is not my concern, nor should it be anyone else's concern, whether or not anyone's soul accepts or rejects God, my role is to prepare for my chance to say YES, YES, YES!

My prayer for this 9th devotional, is that everyone who reads today's offering will search for verses in the Bible that support this point-of-view rather than looking for ways in which "I am (this author is) wrong." I personally have found over 300 New Testament, Epistle, and Old Testament Quotes that support this idea! Please do a little searching of your own. Amen

Day 10

A Devotional for Understanding and Acceptance

Are we responsible for the sad state of our World's Environment?

"And I brought you into a plentiful land to enjoy its fruits and its good things. But when you came in, you defiled my land and made my heritage an abomination." Jeremiah 2:7 Is it not enough for you to feed on the good pasture, that you must tread down with your feet the rest of your pasture; and to drink of clear water, that you must muddy the rest of the water with your feet? Ezekiel 34:18 The earth mourns and withers; the world languishes and withers; the highest people of the earth languish. The earth lies defiled under its inhabitants; for they have transgressed the laws, violated the statutes, broken the everlasting covenant. Therefore, a curse devours the earth, and its inhabitants suffer for their guilt; therefore the inhabitants of the earth are scorched, and few men are left. Isaiah 24:4-6

"When you besiege a city for a long time, making war against it in order to take it, you shall not destroy its trees by wielding an axe against them. You may eat from them, but you shall not cut them down. Are the trees in the field human, that they should be besieged by you? Only the trees that you know are not trees for food you may destroy and cut down, that you may build siegeworks against the city that makes war with you, until it falls." Deuteronomy 20: 19-20 And God said, "Behold, I have given you every plant yielding seed that is on the face of all the earth, and every tree with seed in its fruit. You shall have them for food. And to every beast of the earth and to every bird of the heavens and to everything that creeps on the earth, everything that has the breath of life, I have given every green plant for food." And it was so. Genesis 1: 30

But if anyone has the world's goods and sees his brother in need, yet closes his heart against him, how does God's love abide in him? Little children, let us not love in word or talk, but in deed and in truth. 1 John 3:17-18

For "the earth is the Lord's, and the fullness thereof." 1Corinthians 19:26 "But ask the beasts, and they will teach you; the birds of the heavens, and they will tell you; or the bushes of the earth, and they will teach you; and the fish of the sea will declare to you. Who among all these does not know that the hand of the Lord has done this? In his hand is the life of every living thing and the breath of all mankind. Job 12: 7-10

Why do we create environmental crisis after crisis. We fix one, and new jobs are created as we resolve that problem but then it's on to the next crisis. We don't have to operate this way. This is not how we are supposed to care for God's Creation. If we would stop trying to serve two masters, 1) God and all his creation, and then 2) chasing the "all might $$$$$!" It just does not work. If we all would trust the creative powers of God, we would not want for anything!

Remember this: Look at the birds of the air: they neither sow nor reap nor gather into barns, and yet your heavenly Father feeds them. Are you not of more value than they? Matthew 6:26

Gracious God, we beg forgiveness for not caring for your creation more than we do being right no matter which side of any argument we might be on. You sent Jesus to help us recognize the error in our thinking, and almost every single one of us, these days, believes "YOU COULDN'T have been referring to me, because if anyone knows what you wanted us all to do, because I love you perfectly, no way I could be wrong, Or Could I? I ask for discernment, for me, for my brothers and sisters, and even for those who I presently believe are dead WRONG! I am willing to accept that there is always a chance that I might be wrong, and so could everyone else! Please, forgive us all, because even though it is highly unlikely that we are all correct, it is not inconceivable that we might all have interpreted everything incorrectly! Thank you, God, for allowing us to keep trying. Amen

Day 11

A Devotional for Understanding and Acceptance

How do we know what the truth is?

As we progress through life, we are told so many things by so many people, how do we know what the truth is? One thing we've discovered is that the "truth" is not always so easy to verify. Why is this so? What I view as truth is subjective truth, it's always going to reflect my personal likes, dislikes, fears, areas of expertise, and so many factors that can be influenced by my personal experiences. In experiments that have been repeated with statistically similar results, we see that when something happens, and that event is observed by several people, there will be as many different descriptions of what occurred as there are people making the observations. A few will be fairly close to each other but there will be many that get us wondering if all participants were watch the exact same event.

If we give too much credence to our own memory of an event, we run the risk of believing as much as 50% of what we think we saw is absolutely exactly what transpired, yet very possibly could be fairly distant from what actually took place. How much more distant from reality could what we believe be if the actual events can only be experienced through other people's recollection of what happened. Add to that the possibility that the version we experience was originally based on stories told in a language we do not speak based on a culture that is very different from the culture we live in now. Sometimes, we can even lose the reason these stories were told. When we lose the reason behind the lesson we were supposed to learn, we can put too powerful of a value on some stories and too little value on lessons that should be fundamental guides for our lives.

I have a suggestion for all of us. From this day forward, let's focus on what Jesus clearly stated we should have as the cornerstone of our daily lives.

1. Do not judge, or you too will be judged. For in the same way you judge others, you will be judged, and with the level of severity. Matthew 7: 1-2

2. Truly I tell you, inasmuch as you did it to one of the least of these my brothers, you did it to me. Matthew 25:40

3. Jesus replied, "'You must love the Lord your God with all your heart, all your soul, and all your mind. ' This is the first and greatest commandment. A second is equally important: 'Love your neighbor as yourself. ' The entire law and all the demands of the prophets are based on these two commandments." Matthew: 22:37-40

4. If any one of you is without sin, let him be the first to throw a stone at her. John 8:7

5. Blessed are the poor in spirit, for theirs is the kingdom of heaven. Blessed are those who mourn, for they shall be comforted. Blessed are the meek, for they shall inherit the earth. Blessed are those who hunger and thirst for righteousness, for they shall be satisfied. Blessed are the merciful for they shall receive mercy. Blessed are the pure of heart, for they shall see God. Blessed are the Peacemakers for they shall be called children of God. There's more, but I think you get the idea! Matthew 5:3-12

My prayer is that all who read this will realize that; nowhere in this does Jesus say, Blessed are the rich, powerful, beautiful, and every other marvelous characteristic we all seem to focus on as being what we want to be! That's not why Jesus came to put our lives right with our Creator. I pray that every Christian will finally realize that we must be born again. Which means we are changed into the fundamental person who is described by Jesus in these beatitudes! Amen

Day 12

A Devotional for Understanding and Acceptance

What is Life? What is death? What is non-life?

Are non-living things also non dying things? Is it possible for something that has never been alive to become ALIVE?

The answers to these questions may seem very difficult to discern, but the answers are very easy to figure out. Life and death are truly terms that only apply to complex obrganisms that possess an awareness of their existence. What is meant by awareness? Being aware is having an ability to respond to stimuli that come into our immediate zone of influence. This, in some situations, could be very nearby. So, sunlight hits the leaves of street and the tree produces organic chemicals that they need to maintain their life activities. An earthworm senses excess water in the soil so or in other situations, could be more of a context than a location. I'm not trying to get excessively philosophical or intellectual here. I am, however, suggesting that what seems like awareness in some organisms may not be of much value to another organism. To these other organisms, what is critical knowledge and that knowledge's resulting ability to sense other organisms with either aligned or oppositional needs, might involve significant different qualities, behaviors, and/or styles of engaging in their world.

So all this begs the question, Is God Alive or is God Dead? Was God ever Alive? Does God Exist at all? In the very early days of human civilization, people truly wanted to know how we got here. They made up all sorts of stories to explain where we came from and how we all came into being. For centuries, one group of humans have tried to tell other groups of humans that their god or gods were better than your god or group of gods. Doesn't this all seem a bit immature to you! But we persist to this day to keep telling everyone else that our group has the real Devine Creator and yours? Not so much!

Time marches on and all the while, the power and might of our Benevolent Creator is ignored by the majority of the human population. How do we know that is a true statement? Because the majority of people, more than 4.5 billion of the people 8.2 billion people on this earth either consider themselves Christian, Islamic, or Jewish. These three groups alone make up more than 50% of the world population and, although some variation exists within each group, the people we all constantly hear about are those who have radicalized their faith to suit their own purposes. In the meantime, it feels like we are consistently marching towards a breaking point. As long as we keep arguing about who worships the correct deity, we're lost.

So how do fix this? By understanding that from the very start, God didn't want us to give a name to his divinity! The best name, is **"I AM"** and that is only name we need. **I AM** is not Christian, Jewish, or Muslim. **I AM THAT I AM**, is all cultures, all faiths, all people. **THE GREAT I AM**, sent Jesus not just for those who believed in him, but to all people. Anyone who was not of the Jewish faith was referred to as a gentile; God made all people! If he tiles were not welcome, I am lost, and so are 90% of all the people in the world.

My prayer

I am (so very hopeful) **THAT I AM**, will be so loving, kind, generous, and interested in the salvation of all people, **THAT I AM** will forgives us all for our wrong headedness, hatred for those unlike us, and our willingness to kill those who do not meet our belief matrix. As each person examines their spirit through the Filter of GOD'S Love, let us realize that we are standing on the brink! What will it be? Hatred and Destruction; or Love and Salvation! The choice is ours alone. My choice is Love and Salvation! AMEN!

Day 13

A Devotional for Understanding and Acceptance

If God can heal any disease, injury, or even bring the dead back to life, why do we need doctors? Great question! "For truly I tell you, if you have faith the size of a mustard seed, you will say to this mountain, 'Move from here to there,' and it will move; and nothing will be impossible for you." Matthew 27:20/21

That's the crux of the matter. We don't have the faith even 1/10th the size of a tiny mustard seed, and that requires extra attention from Humans who've been trained to reduce pain, set broken bones, invent chemicals that kill bacteria or viruses, and/or reduce the impact of a variety of environmental and genetic conditions.

Why do I say this? Why do I think, we've brought all of this on ourselves. Here's my evidence.

1. We (I) constantly check to see if our prayers were answered. If I have faith, I know my prayers will be answered, so there is no need to check.

2. Do I think I know what the best answer to each prayer is? Really? How many times are we initially very disappointed, but later on,

when we've forgotten about the details of our prayer request, something very positive happens and we fail to see the connection between our prayer and the positive outcomes we experience.

3. Are we (am I) constantly thinking of ourselves (myself) when we I) pray? Even when we (I) pray for others, are we (am I) seeking results that are best for who we are praying for or are we easing our own sensibilities and hoping for personal comfort?

4. Truly abundant people are extremely generous. People who truly operate from the realm of "Fear of Lacking Enough to 'Survive' (which is a state of existence that is unrealistic) tend to be very selfish!"

5. We allow what we think we need, must have, or really really enjoy, be determined by our past experiences, good or bad, rather than controlling how we conduct our lives based on love, joy, and the amazing gift we've been given!

6. Ask yourself this question: what has Jesus asked me to do? His brother, James tells us that if we have faith but act in a way that doesn't honor God and Jesus, and the Spirit that binds us all together, do we really have faith? "For as the body without the spirit is dead, so faith without works is dead also." James 2:26

You may disagree with my thoughts and analysis, that is your right as a human being. But if you disagree, please ask yourself the question in #6 above and answer that question in the same way Jesus would. My goal is to get as close to the spirit of the living God as I possibly can! Lead me My Beautiful Savior on this path I walk!

Day 14

A Devotional for Understanding and Acceptance

How can we Rejoice in this World Gone MAD?

Rejoice and be thankful, always! "Rejoice always; pray continually; give thanks in all circumstances, for this is God's will for you in Christ Jesus." 1 Thessalonians 5:16-18 Wait a minute! This can't be right. I'm supposed to be thankful in all circumstances? Really? If someone I love dearly is harmed or killed, I'm so supposed to be thankful! That's crazy.

Well, when you put it that way, from that perspective; yes, that's crazy. But God is not crazy. God is not asking us to be thankful for these bad things that have happened. No, he wants you to remember that there is always something to be thankful for. If a loved one is hurt or even killed, we can be thankful for the love that was shown to us by that loved one. Why should we focus on that love we can be thankful for. Love, gratitude, and joy are healing emotions and can be used to help carry forward with our lives, even during the most negative times and circumstances.

If we spend our time focused on what hurt us, we can miss the good that still exists in our world. Today the news was filled with the passing if Lisa Marie Presley. The news reporters declared that the daughter of Elvis never got over her son's suicide. By focusing on what was taken from her, she experienced pain, anguish, and depression. This affected her health and reduced her will to live. By focusing on what you do not have, we ignore our blessings. And those blessings give us the energy and drive to go on with our lives. By remembering everything that we have, helps us understand that we are loved by many people, Jesus, and our God.

This is very hard, but so very necessary. What hurts us is outside our soul. What heals us, and truly makes us happy is inside our soul. There is no thing, no body, no-one, no-action, no building, no-place, no-time, NO-EXPERIENCE, outside our Spirit/Soul as it connects to our Creator that can bring us true happiness. There's this concept of Let Go and Let God! But most of us want God to supply before we will let Go. If we stand on the shore, clinging to what we know, can feel, and have experienced, we can never sail the seas. You must trust God's love enough to put your life fully in his hands! Let Go! Have Faith! Once you have that faith, God will move mountains to show the Love that is already in you.

Love is patient and kind. Love is not jealous or boastful or proud or rude. It does not demand its own way. It is not irritable, and it keeps no record of being wronged. It does not rejoice about injustice but rejoices whenever the truth wins out. Love never gives up, never loses faith, is always hopeful, and endures through every circumstance. (1 Corinthians 13:4-7) Such love has no fear, because perfect love expels all fear. If we are afraid, it is for fear of punishment, and this shows that we have not fully experienced His perfect love. (1 John 4:18) And I am convinced that nothing can ever separate us from God's love. Neither death nor life, neither angels nor demons, neither our fears for today nor our worries about tomorrow — not even the powers of hell can separate us from God's love. Romans 8:37-38

God, my eternal parent, creator of heavens and earth, help me to love as I have been loved. Fill me with the spirit of love! Fill me with the love Christ has for me! As we walk through this life, let us not forget that: "No power in the sky above or in the earth below — indeed, nothing in all creation will ever be able to separate us from the love of God that is revealed in Christ Jesus our Lord." Romans 8:39 Amen

Day 15

A Devotional for Understanding and Acceptance

Is there room for hate in God's creation?

Let's examine what Jesus made quite clear! There are 2 types of Commandments that give meaning to the reason why Jesus came to Save Mankind! Jesus told us, that he did not come to abolish the Law but to fulfill it. Why was this a reasonable answer when he was asked why he allowed his disciples to violate one of the 10 Commandments; # 4 which tells us to Remember the Sabbath and keep it Holy. Jesus knew why these laws were created. They were created out of love. There are 2 types of Commandments: 1-3 are all about Loving God with #1 Heart (Put nothing above me (God). Exodus 20:3), #2 Spirit (Don't worship idols: Golden things, great paintings, silver service pieces, or, $$$$. Exodus 20:4) and #3 Mind (Don't defame or profane The Creator or God's Creation, Exodus 20: 7).

Commandments 4-10 tell us all the things we might do that demonstrate a huge lack of love for other people. Any one of these can cause disruption of peace in a community, region, and/or nation. #4: The sabbath is about bosses not overworking their employees/servants-not about allowing people to meet their daily needs. Exodus 20:7 #5 Honor those who cared for you as you grew, learned, and developed (for most fortunate people, those are mom and dad) Exodus 20:12 #6 Don't kill, Exodus 20:13 which means to intentionally end people's lives either through actions taken or actions not taken. #7 Do not cheat on your husband or wife. exodus 20:14 #8 Do not take things that do not belong to you Exodus 20:15 #9 Don't tell things about someone else that you know are not nor can it be verified as truth. Exodus 20:16 #10 Do not covet (excessively desire) what other people have. Exodus 20:17

So when Jesus says "I did not come to abolish the law but to fulfill it," (Matthew 5:17) he is saying I know why Moses came down from The Mountain with these laws, and why the prophets and Rabbis had to keep clarifying what these 10 laws meant. It's not about controlling people; it was about how we best express love to God and all of God's Creation.

Another way we can show a serious lack of love for God and the people he created, is to adhere to any of these commandments out of context. These Commands were given to the Israelites because they too often forgetting who they were and who created them. These failures often brought dishonor to God's people and too often drive people away from considering God's Love. In their overzealous efforts to control people, and often for disingenuous reasons, some Hebrews led those they didn't like from Worshiping their God, who was, not just their God but the Creator of all.

Tomorrow, I will challenge you to look beyond our narrow interpretation of many laws and thoughts that are creating anguish and distress in our modern world. My prayer is that we will have a quiet spirit, open mind, and loving heart as we continue to look for Understanding and Acceptance. Amen

Day 16

A Devotional for Understanding and Acceptance

What is the difference between Faith and Belief?

What you think continuously, day in and day out will reveal what you truly believe. How you behave is a result of how much faith you have in what you believe. There are many people who profess Christianity as their as their guiding belief, yet lack the faith in God and Jesus, to allow the spirit that connects them to one another, and ultimately to every living thing, including those professing to be followers of Christ, to be the real guide for everything they do. A few days ago, I posed the question that asked : is God Alive or is God Dead. My faith is in the Spirit of the Living God which no life can exist without. As James (2:13) states: The body without God's spirit is dies, just as faith with doing anything to show how our faith can improve life for all people was never truly a living faith!

Yesterday, I told you that this Devotional would challenge you to take a look at "how narrow are our interpretations of the laws that govern our behaviors?" The Christian Church has been divided for most its existence by what sacred writings we use as a basis for the laws we follow, how we interpret the laws, and which laws, of the hundreds of laws that we find in our Holy Books, we should follow, and which can and should ignore. We often hear that there are immutable, inviolable laws of nature, that are too awful for humans to ignore, nor should we ever tolerate breaking these abominations. One of these notions has to do with Gender identity. How could we possibly ignore biological facts?

What are biological facts? Here are my thoughts on this one aspect of what many people are getting quite angry with and have very specific beliefs about. Let's start out with a question.

"What does Gender identify have to do with our Creator God!" In a perfect world, it would be totally irrelevant. However, we do not live in a perfect world. This has resulted in humans, who do not understand simple biological principles, but keep trying to speak for God! Some people actually think gender matters to the Creator of the Universe! Gender is only important for reproduction. If it mattered, there would not be a single solitary organism that would be anything other than a male or a female. There are male flowers (as recognized by having a gamete that travels to fertilize another gamete) and female flowers which have that gamete awaiting fertilization. However, there are flowers that have both male and female reproductive parts. And this happens in many other species, by design in some, such as earthworms and in by accident in others such as dolphins, colobus monkeys, spotted hyenas, Marsh

Harriers (a small marsh raptor), and human beings. There are some animal species that can change from male to female as needed by their local population. As we learn more and more about what effects genetic change over time, we've realized that genetic expression of a wide range of characteristics depends on more than just having a specific set of genes that have been passed on.

A new area of genetic study and research has emerged over the past few decades. The emerging field of "Epigenetic" studies help us understand how external (outside each organism) and internal (inside any individual organism) environmental conditions can either suppress the expression of some genes or activate the expression of genes and whether a specific set of genes will stimulate or inhibit the production of proteins that cause either helpful or harmful traits. So, then there are humans. For thousands of years, humanity has dealt with issues related to gender expression. For the last few hundred years, we've taken our lack of understanding to an excessive extreme. Biblically, the only references we see deal almost exclusively with men forcing other men to perform acts against their will. Today, we forget the context of the biblical condemnation of those acts. These were acts done out of disrespect for specific groups of people and unwanted foreigners in their land. How would Jesus approach those present-day Violators of the ancient laws? I believe he would say let the person among all of those, who is without sin, and who are accusing the "Wong doer" flip the switch , lock the door behind the perpetrator, Condemn the person to hell. If this was a requirement for everyone sitting on the judge's bench or in a jury box, there would be a whole lot less people being convicted of serious crimes. Why are we spending so much of our human energy on issues that truly don't matter.

In fact, the Ancient world had ways to terminate a pregnancy that is a result of behavior that is not acceptable to the wife and/or her husband. What might those circumstances be? Adultery, Rape, Incest, are just three of the things that I can see that might lead to a desired termination. 3,000 years ago, the world population put very little stress on the ability of our planet to produce everything we need for species survival. But even then, more value was placed on the life of a woman than on an unborn child. Today, our world has more people consuming excessive resources and producing excessive waste. God does not want us to destroy our world. He created it, and it is very difficult to imagine that God wouldn't want us to do everything we can to preserve creation.

Today's Prayer:

Holy God, Creator of everything, help us all examine our motivations for why we do things we do while invoking your name and saying we do this in your name. Your Child, Jesus, whom you sent to help us figure all these legal issues out, spent very little, if any, of the time allotted to teach us, focused on so many of these issues we seem to put so much emphasis on! Why do we do this while ignoring the issues Jesus wanted us to spend our time, energy, and faith on! Creator God, Creator Child of God, and High Energy Spirit of the Creator, please, we explore you, forgive our unwillingness to bend to your will, and lead us on word towards allowing the True Word of God to raise us all up to become all you want us to become. Amen

Day 17

A Devotional for Understanding and Acceptance

When I try to list for God's Voice, why can't I heart him?

God does not speak to us in a spoken language. God speaks to us using the power and energy used in the creative act. Energy is transmitted in waves, such as light (vision), sound (words, music, or other noises), warmth, sensations, etc! We were told to seek and you shall find, knock and the door will be opened to you, ask it shall be given! Yet, many of us seek and do not know what we've found, knocked on a door but it's the wrong door, or have asked and been surprised by what we've received!

We never stop to think that what keeps us from receiving what we "hoped" we would receive, is the tower of obstructionist, off target, totally misaligned, negatively oriented statements of what we do not want rather than clearly state what we truly desired from the very start! This causes us to inadvertently create a blockage which prevents our reception of the gifts waiting for us. So how do we come to understand what God says to us? Much can be learned from reading and paying careful attention to what Jeshua (Jesus) taught his disciples. More can be learned from praying from our HEARTS, not our brains or egos. Once AGAIN, after we have studied and prayed, we should meditate! Here is a process for mediation that I use at least once every day. I sit comfortably (I use my most comfortable chair); I close my eyes; I focus my mind on a continuous, unremarkable sound (I use a box fan that makes a continuous low vibrational hum); while you are listening to the sound, your mind may wander—that's ok but you want to Get your mind back to the focus, so you need a trigger! I use the thought of a Joyful Noise. So, if I feel I've wavered from my focus, I think about my favorite Joyful noise and I return to the focus; Set a timer for 20 minutes; If nothing happens in 20 minutes, try again tomorrow! Jot down, in as few words as possible, what you experienced!

My Prayer: Gracious God, help us all to find the joyful noise in the world around us. Let us see the beauty that is there and remind us of all we have to be grateful for. We pray for all those who need healing; all those who need comfort; and all those who need a kind word. Help us remember to be your voice, feet, and hands in this world and help us provide the comfort and love so many need in these troubled times. AMEN

Day 18

A Devotional for Understanding and Acceptance

What Good is Gratitude?

Take time to be grateful! Think of all that God has done for you! You may believe, from time to time, that "Life is so hard, I'm not sure I can go on!" Believe me, if you will listen for the voice of God in the world around you, you will be amazed. A grateful heart, will lead to more happiness than you might possibly imagine. This begins the journey! God will not save those who openly reject the connection between his spirit and one's own. When Jesus said the "kingdom of God is at hand," (Mark 1:15) he truly meant it! It is not on some far away plain, in the hands of another, found in the actions of others, nor can it be bought. It is here, right here, right now! Each of us must take the very simple step of ACCEPTANCE! God's Kingdom is open to all, yes even you, no matter who you are, what you have done, where you have been, or what you presently believe. If you will truly, without hesitation or any conditionality, accept this fact, your life will be forever changed. The change will be as if you've sloughed off your old worldly body and now, you are brand new, being. This is the easiest thing in the world to do. Simply accept the gift. But, there are too many people that want us to "BE

GOOD!" Jesus would not have been necessary if we could be good enough. If keeping every, or even one or two rules made us all righteous in the EYES of GOD, what was the reason for Jesus' Sacrifice. The work is done! We have nothing more to do but accept the amazing Grace of God. This gift has no strings attached. It's ours for the simple act of accepting the gift. Once you've truly accepted the gift, your old life is gone and you will experience the new life. Rejoice in the DAY THE LORD HAS MADE! Be Grateful! Hallelujah Peace to all!

Thank you for loving me, saving me, and for teaching me to be kind. Your love is so powerful; you loved me when I could not even love myself. You taught me that anger, hatred, and discontent are bitter pills we force ourselves to hold in our mouths, hoping they will become sweet nectar but we swallow them and our anger increases. The only way to healing is to immediately spit out the bitter pills of hatred, anger, and discontent. Allow the sweet honey and nectar of goodness into our lives and watch the transformation begin. Let me love, accept, honor, and learn better ways to live.

Lord, make me an instrument of your peace, where there is hatred, let me sow love, where there is injury, pardon, where there is doubt, faith, where there is despair, hope, where there is darkness, light, and where there is sadness, joy.

O Divine Master, grant that I may not so much seek, to be consoled as to console, to be understood as to understand, to be loved as to love, For it is in giving that we receive, it is in pardoning that we are pardoned, and it is in dying that we are born to eternal life.

Amen.

—St. Francis of Assisi

Now set a timer for 20 minutes and let's take some time to reflect on our lives. Let's Meditate. Put on some gentle, soft sound or music and just let your mind wander. If you start thinking about what you have to do, or if bad thoughts enter your mind: Take a deep breath, then breathe in for a count of 5 (this is the YAH)—hold your breath for a count of 4, exhale to a count of 8, (this is the WEH) and repeat these 5 to 7 times. As soon as you've calmed your mind, start again. After you've meditated, jot down a few notes about the experience. Don't worry if you don't feel any better after today's session. Remember God Loves You, and so do we.

Day 19

A Devotional for Understanding and Acceptance

Why can't God just make us behave?

And the journey continues! Some people will begin to experience some alterations in their spiritual suit after a few days of devotion and regular meditation. Others may take quite a bit longer. The difficulty, or ease with which you begin to feel a transformation begin, solidify, grow, and continue to make an ever-expanding impact on how you view and experience "your personal connection to God and all of creation, depends of 3 critical understandings.

1.   First, that it is not God's responsibility to get you to love "God, One Another, and All of Creation;" That is your responsibility.

2.   Second, it is not your responsibility to do anything at all to be worthy of God's Love for you; he already has, does, and will continue to do so.

3.   Third, it is the responsibility of each member of the human race to love the "self," (individual and collective), all others, and the totality of creation and the Creator that set it all in motion.

There is Great NEWS! We do not hate nearly as much as many people think "WE" do. Truth is, we knee-jerk react to things that scare us, and then justify our actions of fear and cowardice because we just can't trust those things that just seem so "WAY OUT THERE! SO BIZARRE! THINGS THAT ARE NOT ACCEPTABLE IN OUR SOCIETY! But, just off the top of your head, who did Jesus come to help?

Jesus wasn't about saving the brightest, strongest, richest, or most clever! God does not need to help those who help themselves. I challenge anyone to find a quote anywhere that says God helps those that help themselves. Our Savior came for those who had been beaten, starved, thrown into prison, bonded into slavery, sick, and dejected. He constantly reminded us that he who wants to be first but be last. He wasn't really saying he's going to pull you out of line and send you all the way to the end of the line. He was simply pointing out that the person he admires most is the person who makes sure everyone else's needs are met before greatest among us will Allie themselves to be served.

And in that day, the king will ask, "when I was sick or imprisoned did you come visit me? When I was starving and thirsty, did you feed me or give me drink? When I was exhausted and heartbroken did you give me a place to rest or console me?" You may ask: when did I see you in any of these states and not provide to you what you required? And the king will reply, "as you have or have not done for the most insignificant human being, in that measure you have done it to me!" Matthew 25:44-45

Tonight, you may need meditation more than ever! Peace be in your every waking moment! Sit comfortably (I use my most comfortable chair); close your eyes; focus your mind on a continuous, unremarkable sound (I use a box fan that makes a continuous low vibrational hum); while you are listening to the sound, your mind may wander— that's ok but you want to get back to the focus, so you need a trigger! I use the thought of A Joyful Noise. So, if I feel I've wavered from my focus, I think about my favorite Joyful noise and I return to the focus; Set a timer for 20 minutes; If nothing happens in 20 minutes, try again tomorrow! Jot down, in as few words as possible, what you experienced!

My Prayer: Gracious God teach us how to meditate on your word and help us to avoid distractions. Teach us to love as you have loved us and teach us to care for others as you have cared for us. Bless these days of struggle with your comfort and love and help us to always keep your Son, Jesus in our hearts. AMEN

Day 20

A Devotional for Understanding and Acceptance

Am I too Much like Pharaoh?

Most people recognize that if they want life to be better, they themselves need to be better. The difficulty arises when they realize that who they are, at this very moment in time, can never get better. Jesus knew this. That's why John related this story "Now there was a man of the Pharisees named Nicodemus, a member of the Jewish ruling council. He came to Jesus at night and said, 'Rabbi, we know you are a teacher who has come from God. For no one could perform the miraculous signs you are doing if God were not with him.' In reply Jesus declared, 'I tell you the truth, no one can see the kingdom of God unless he is born again.' 'How can a man be born when he is old' Nicodemus asked. 'Surely he cannot enter a second time into his mother's womb to be born!' Jesus answered, 'I tell you the truth, no one can enter the kingdom of God unless he is born of water and the Spirit. Flesh gives birth to flesh, but the Spirit gives birth to spirit. You should not be surprised at my saying, You must be born again.'" John 3:1-7

What Jesus teaches all who will listen, the only way to be a better person is to become a spiritual person. You cannot remain who you presently are! How will we know if a person transitions from an earthly/body-oriented person into a Spiritual Person. It's very easy to see a Spiritual Person when you compare that person to a person in the bodily focused realm!

My Father's house has many rooms; if that were not so, would I have told you that I am going there to prepare a place for you? And if I go and prepare a place for you, I will come back and take you to be with me so that you also may be where I am. John,14:2-3

In God, whose word I praise, in God I trust; I will not be afraid. What can mortal man do to me? — Psalm 56:

Earthly Focused **People**	**Spiritually Focused People**
Emotional base: conditional love, anger towards unworthy people, hate for people who refuse to conform	Emotional Base: Unconditional Love and Compassion
Basis for faith: because I profess my faith, I am saved	Basis for faith: The only salvation attainable is by accepting a gift No one is capable of earning
Behavior based on the right way for Christians to behave.	Behavior based on **Love** and **Compassion**, not rules and laws.
Disgusted by people who refuse to conform to my standards.	Love and compassion shown to all people, no questions asked, no conditions, no prerequisites.

Lord Jesus, as you have so carefully taught us, yet we have hardened our hearts and resisted. We have not been terribly unlike Pharaoh: Moses and Aaron went in, and told Pharaoh, the Lord God of Israel says, Let my people go, so "they may hold a feast to celebrate me" in the wilderness. Exodus 5:1 Then the Lord God said to Moses, "You are to say everything I command you; and your brother Aaron is to tell Pharaoh to let the Israelites go out of his country." But Pharaoh's heart, was hardened, and though God multiplied his signs and wonders in Egypt, Pharaoh would not listen to The "Word of God." Exodus 7: 2-4 Dear Jesus, help all of us keep our Hearts open, compassionate, and full of your UNCONDITIONAL LOVE! Our world now needs the Love of Jesus more than ever before! Amen

Day 21

A Devotional for Understanding and Acceptance

How can I rebalance my life?

As we proceed through the days we have, we will win and we will lose on this journey. I've heard some very wise people say we need the loses so that we can fully appreciate the victories! Sometimes those losses are so difficult to take, it can take quite a while to recover. The death of a child or a spouse can knock us off balance. We might think, how can we ever get back to a balanced life. (Question: are we ever really in a Balanced State?) That loved one helped us see the potholes in life that we now seem to constantly step in. How can I rebalance my life?

2,000 years ago, during the days Jesus experienced life as a human, many of the spiritual practices of our present day world, could be experienced within a few hundred miles of one another. They were intermingled without concern. It is quite evident that Jesus was well aware of these various ways to be in contact with God through a more spiritual self. Getting away from the hustle of everyday life to center oneself on one's relationship with the Creator was something Jesus did on a regular basis. We hear so much about being "WOKE" and it has set off firestorms of controversy. I believe, that if compare Jesus' concept of being fully alive to what people refer to as being "WOKE," you will see incredible similarities between the roots of the two concepts. Jesus says: "John 10:10, **The thief comes only to steal and kill and destroy; I have come that they may have life and have it to the full.**" In other words, Jesus came so that be FULLY ALIVE!

Originally, WOKE was a term used by African Americans to remind them to be "Fully aware" of the political, social, and environmental issues that are happening all around "US!" It included past, present, and future issues of discrimination, abuse, and all types of conditions faced on a daily basis. It more recently has become a rallying point for both ends of the political spectrum. It should be a rallying cry for all who Love Christ. To be WOKE, should be a requirement for achieving a Life Fully Lived! To experience the ABUNDANT LIFE of a true FOLLOWER OF CHRIST, we should all be concerned about how the least of these are treated.

I propose that we adopt a new Term to Replace WOKE! That Term is "Fully Aware" of my Responsibility as a Follower of Christ for doing everything I can to make sure that I help and never harm. "Fully Aware" of harm done in the past and doing everything I can to recognize that harm and assist those affected to get past the harm and move forward toward a more successful future. "Fully Aware" that what any other person has experienced, either personally or through being placed in a disadvantageous situation, is real to that person and should be honored. "Fully Aware" that the best way to move forward for our entire society is for every citizen to take the time to help everyone who feels disadvantaged have the opportunity to experience success. My personal experience tells me, the vast majority of people want three things: 1. To be respected, 2. To be listened to, and 3. To know the key to success lies within reach.

Therefore, as we have opportunity, let us do good to all people, especially to those who belong to the family of believers. Galatians 6:10

"Then he said, 'This is what I'll do. I will tear down my barns and build bigger ones, and there I will store my surplus grain. And I'll say to myself, "You have plenty of grain laid up for many years. Take life easy; eat, drink and be merry."'"

"But God said to him, 'You fool! This very night your life will be demanded from you. Then who will get what you have prepared for yourself?' "This is how it will be with whoever stores up things for themselves but is not rich toward God." Luke 12:18-21

Thank you, Amazing Creator, you have guided us to be fully alive and Fully Aware. Help me fulfill this expectation even though we live in a world full of excessively hardened hearts! Amen

Day 22

A Devotional for Understanding and Acceptance

Is there any person who is so incredibly different or vile that they are undeserving of your Love?

Obviously, men and women are significantly different, just as there are huge differences between Blacks, Whites, and People from south of the Rio Grande! There's no way anyone could ever think they are but one type! We hear so much about how we are so different. We are a divided nation: Republican, Democrat, Immigrants, Northerner, Southerner, Urban, Suburban, Country Bumpkin, everyone unique with incredible differences which separates us by our beliefs, loyalties, and religious leanings.

For the Son of Man came to seek and to save the lost. Luke 19:10 which of the people above are lost? That is a matter of perspective!

For God did not send his Son into the world to condemn the world, but to save the world through him. John 3:17 Therefore, even if you think another person, because of their skin color, ethnicity, past behaviors, political beliefs, religion or lack there of, it is never our place to condemn that person!

After this I looked, and there before me was a great multitude that no one could count, from every nation, tribe, people and language, standing before the throne and before the Lamb. They were wearing white robes and were holding palm branches in their hands. Revelations 7:9 It doesn't take any wild imagination to realize that John, in what was reveals to him, clearly states what too many want to deny. That Christ is the savior of all people, from every corner of the world! What did they do to deserve this? They are part of God's Creation. To receive this Gift, each person must simply accept it. And as hard as that is for some very Legalistically minded people to understand, All means All, All except! No one who accepts the gift will have it taken away! The Gift changes lives forever!

Dear Creator of us all, thank you for loving me; a good old 57 varieties type human being. When states (that there is neither Jew nor Greek, slave nor free, male nor female, for you are all one in Christ Jesus. — Galatians 3:28) it gives such comfort and peace. Let's all go forward from this day till the end of all time, sowing love and abandoning any remnant of hate we might find on our journey. Amen

Day 23

A Devotional for Understanding and Acceptance

What is meant by the sins of the father?

The Old Testament has passages in Exodus, Deuteronomy, and Numbers that address how the indiscretion of parents can impact generations. But is this really what God wants for us? I think, we do it to ourselves. The law as given to the ancient Hebrews was a series of warnings to the faithful as to what could lead to major difficulties should they behave in a way that most of society would find intolerable. Let me give you a personal example.

Recently, I've been working with the Women's Basketball at Western Michigan University. There are many minor differences between between championship teams and perennial non-championship teams. As I work to help our players create the inner drive, confidence, and mental consistency to narrow the gap, I have found meditation as a tool to build inner strength. I was engaged in a meditation led by Kelly Boys, a mindfulness trainer. She was helping us find our safe place. She asked us to think about a time, when we felt safe. She wanted us to describe the conditions that were integral to that feeling of safety. As I thought through my experiences, I realized that I was going to have difficulty finding that experience. I'm not blaming, but trying to understand why. My great grandmother Sarah Newman was a hard woman who put extraordinary pressure on her 7 children. My grandfather, who was 11 when his father passed away in 1907, enlisted in the fledgling Army Air corp during WWI, just days after my Great grandmother had forbid him from enlisting. I won't go into how he was treated when finally got home in late 1919. But the bitterness he experienced from his own Mother, he passed on to his only child, my Dad.

So, when my Dad got married and had kids, the 4 of us kids walked on Egg Shells continuously. Later, I realized our mom was in the boat! My safe spot was a place I came to after college, when I married Barb, and we had 3 marvelous kids. That safe place was in the home of my in-laws, Jack and Marilyn Joynt! The love, care, and positivity they brought my family was life changing. There were 3 generations of misery and my sister's life ended at the age of 28, under questionable circumstances after a brief, abusive marriage. My younger brother has had a tumultuous life. So, there reasonably could be considered another 1/2 generation.

So, when we read that: "You shall not bow yourself down to them, nor serve them. For I, the Lord your God am a jealous God, visiting the iniquity of the fathers upon the sons to the third and fourth generation of those who hate Me, and doing mercy to thousands of those who love Me and keep My commandments" Deuteronomy 5: 9-10 To me, what this means can be seen in the lives of members of many, many families. Those who wander from the positive path that Jesus lights up for us to follow, don't only harm themselves but, the next few generations as well. You may have heard it said that "the Apple doesn't fall too far from the tree."

My prayer is this: "Creator of all that is Good and Holy, please help us end the cycle of hate, distrust, violence, substance abuse, child abuse, spousal abuse, and all manner of deceit and evil. I pray that, these individuals will find their way back to the path that Jesus has laid out for us. Too often, those of us who have struggled don't even know why we struggle and it will take a major intervention by someone who is willing to risk so much to save us! Thankfully, that's why you sent Jesus to us, for "Once I was lost but now I'm found; was Blind but now I see!" Amen

Day 24

A Devotional for Understanding and Acceptance

Jealousy: is this the real original sin?

The Apostle Paul wrote in his letter to the Galatians (6:4) "Let each person examine their own work. Then each individual can take pride in what they do and not compare their work with someone else." This is the core of jealousy.

"But if you have bitter envy and selfish ambition in your heart, don't brag and deny the truth. Such wisdom does not come from above but is earthly, unspiritual, demonic. For where envy and selfish ambition exist, there is disorder and every kind of evil." James 3:14-16

"And I saw that all toil and all achievement spring from one person's envy of another. This too is meaningless, a chasing after the wind." Ecclesiastes 4:4

Why are we so jealous? Why do we want what others have? Cars, houses, jobs, talent, clothes, beauty, even spouses; these can drive us to do what is unimaginable when a world is focused on scarcity. The sources of jealousy can become reasons for manipulation, murder, theft, discrimination, adultery, slavery, deceit and so many other horrible behaviors. Last night I dreamt that I was required to share something I truly loved with my brother. If my brother hadn't been such jealous sort, he would not have desired what I had! But, why would I have this dream when I never had more than he did? Then it dawned on me, I am the one who always wanted what my brother had. As a result, I often blamed him for too many of the problems I faced and attributed many things he did as being selfish oneupmanship. I never liked the musical ANNIE GET YOUR GUN! The song "Anything You can do, I can do Better," was a constant rebuke of my inability to be #1!

Afterward the LORD asked Cain, "Where is your brother? Where is Abel?" "I don't know," Cain responded. "Am I my brother's keeper?" Genesis 4:9 So it began, Cain tried to blame Abel for his own shortcomings and then justified his behavior through asking why should I be responsible for that guy? So am I my brother's keeper? "But he who is joined to the Lord becomes one spirit with him." 1 Corinthians 6:17 So ask yourself, is Jesus my brother's keeper? If Jesus is your brother's keeper, and if your spirit is joined to the Lord Jesus and his Spirit, can we ever not be responsible for everything that happens to our brothers and sisters?

Gracious Lord, Jealousy may not be the ORIGINAL Sin, but it has probably been responsible for almost every sin committed by every human being since the dawn of time. I know for certain it has been the cause of my discontent! I ask that you forgive my sins! Spirit of the living God, Fall afresh on me. **Spirit of the living God, Fall afresh on me. Break me, melt me, Mold me, fill me. Spirit of the living God, Fall afresh on me. Amen**

Day 25

A Devotional for Understanding and Acceptance

Are You a Realist, a pessimist, or are you a Positivity Focused Human?

I've been chastised by people because I've tried to be an extremely positive person! The power of being positive is incredibly transformational and truly can change every aspect of any person's life. However, for way too many people, this is like scraping my fingernails across their personal proverbial chalkboard.

You might be one of the people who ask, what wrong with being a realist? I have a very simple answer to that question. There's nothing wrong with being a realist, as long as you understand that the reality you adhere to is entirely dependent upon you mindset. What's real is not what other people say or what might happen in a month if 30 things go wrong. Reality is entirely what **YOU DECIDE WHAT YOUR REALITY IS.** Reality is always what you say it is, but you must understand that your reality is only your reality! Your reality is not my reality and therefore, I am not subject to, or bound by the lack of abundance contained in your reality. Your reality can be based on what's going on at this very minute, or what has happened in the past, or it can be generated as a new experience on a continuous basis.

Here are 2 very different realities that both had roots in someone else's Reality. In college, our football team had 2 quarterbacks. One quarterback set records for passing yards, completion percentage, and touchdown passes at his high school in the north suburbs f Chicago. The other was a quarterback whose coach ran a single wing offense in high school and threw les than 20 passes per season completed most of them, and his team won most of their games and were conference champions in 1966. After their freshman year at our Division 3 college, the guy who threw, perhaps 30 passes in 3 years in high school, was named starting quarterback at our college. In fact Ken was so good, he was drafted in the 3rd round by the Cincinnati Bengals. Kenny Anderson set the record for completion percentage in the NFL in 1982; 70.6%. That record stood until 2009, when it was broken by Drew Brees of the Saints.

Nobody thought Ken could throw a football, so he was ignored by every Division 1 and 2 football program in the country. The best quarterback at Northwestern during Ken's years at Augustana was Maurice Daigneau. And at the University of Illinois, there were 2 quarterbacks that found their way to the NFL, after playing at Illinois. Bob Napolic signed with the Houston Oilers, and lasted a very short time.

So who was the other QB at Augustana. He was a very nice guy! I knew him well. He played baseball for 1 year after his sophomore year but after that year he was done with spurts at Augie. Everybody thought he would be one of the best ever at Augie but Ken, was in another league. He never let anyone tell him he wasn't good enough. Or maybe with your size you should be a tight end.

Don't let people do that to you, put you on a pedestal like that. (or knock you off the path) You all have a single Teacher, and you are all classmates. Don't set people up as experts over your life, letting them tell you what to do. Matthew 13:14

Don't let others define you. Be your own person. You truly can be anything you decide to be. You are unlimited! God wants you to be what the world needs more of! Positive, kind, loving and most of all a benefit for all mankind! Thank you Amazing, Wonderful Creator. I count my blessings every day! My spirit soars with the wings of eagles and my life if full with abundance I am unable to number! Please share your bounty with the entire world by helping every single person in the world to be the positive realists we know they can and should be! Amen

Day 26

A Devotional for Understanding and Acceptance

Who is responsible for making things right with all those who have been oppressed?

Our Youth must fight a continuous, uphill battle! Society keeps telling them how much the world is changing and that it will be their responsibility to make sense of it all and put things "RIGHT!" Who will tell us what is right? How will today's Youth figure what is really right?

If they listen closely to the elders of today, they would have us believe that we can simply return to the values and ethics of America's past, and they will be able to find their way. What was ethical behavior in our Country when we first started the Great American Experiment? It was perfectly ethical for our European ancestors to own and treat their African slaves any way they pleased. And then, today, it's ok to insist that the descendants of these enslaved people should "just get over it!"At the same time, many Americans feel our rights have been infringed because we were asked (yes sometimes required) to wear a mask in public places during the Covid 19 pandemic. We even protested when we were required to be vaccinated if we wanted to keep our jobs if we worked in positions that potentially put us in contact with vulnerable people! Which is worse, being owned and sold like livestock or being required to wear a mask and be vaccinated if you might spread a deadly disease.

I will admit that after the attack on 9/11, I thought it was appropriate to restrict the rights of people from predominantly Islamic Countries. I knew both of my sons would be involved in war to stop those that held so little respect for the lives of those innocent people who died in the World Trade Center, The Pentagon, and on that field in Pennsylvania. But it didn't take very long for me to realize that punishing every Muslim was a very unfair, unethical approach to the problem. But there are still many, millions in fact, that still believe all Muslims are bad and should never be allowed to hold office in the US!

Many people have intentionally told bold face lies to sway public opinion in their favor! These same people have fabricated so many lies over the years that they now believe they must have witnessed or at least had a family member experience these atrocities in the World Trade Center, Baghdad, on the border in Texas, and at the ballot box. Who's right and who's wrong? What happened yesterday cannot be changed but our perception and interpretation can.

What would God want from us? There are a very few reasons why anyone would manipulate information they use to lead people. All are covered by 10 Commandments. Coveting others possessions, desiring another's home, job, wife, intelligence, etc: that can lead to all sorts of bad! But all of that can be resolved very easily if we stick to Our Saviors 2 most important commandments: Love God and Love all HUMANKIND! Was it only Jesus and the Apostles that talked about those 2 commandments being so important?

The most famous verse in Leviticus may be the command, **"Love your neighbor as yourself"** Lev. 19:18

Of course, we would not be considered a neighbor to the Jews in the era of Jesus. The only people the Pharisees, Sadducees, and Scribes and Priests thought worthy were the Children of Abraham, the Hebrew or Jewish people. Jesus expanded those worthy to all people! Samaritan, Greek, the clean and unclean, Sinners and Saints alike; male-female, moms, dads, and especially Children! "Who, then, is the greatest in the kingdom of heaven? Jesus called a little child to him and placed the child among them. And he said: Truly I tell you, unless you change and become like little children, you will never enter the kingdom of heaven. Therefore, whoever takes the lowly position of this child is the greatest in the kingdom of heaven. And whoever welcomes one such child in my name welcomes me." Matthew 18:2–5

Gracious Creator Lord, we know that "Hatred stirs up strife, but love covers all offenses." Proverbs 10:12 And that we should "Learn to do good; seek justice, correct oppression; bring justice to the fatherless, and plead the widow's cause. Isaiah 1:17 Even knowing this we mock those we don't understand. We tell the poor, the homeless, the sick, those who have been oppressed: "GET OVER IT!" We owe you nothing. If anyone owed us nothing, it was the Creator and his Omnipresent child in our midst, our savior: Jesus. Because our organizational mess, I fear more people have lost their faith than have acquired a new robust, growing faith. In this age, where so many people no longer turn their face to the creator, and still some well-meaning but nevertheless ill- suited for drawing new believers too Christ, refuse to accept the mantle of love Christ shares with us. Please loving Creator God, forgive our ignorant transgressions of thinking we know better than Jesus. For Jesus was quite clear, no comes to the father except through him: and the only way we can flow through the Jesus Filter is to be pure, unconditional Love! Love God, Love one another, and Love the Journey we are all on together! Amen

Day 27

A Devotional for Understanding and Acceptance

Why do I continuously Self Sabotage my efforts at becoming the best person I can be?

Why is that every time I start making progress, I seem to sabotage myself?

Or I get sick?

Or I just run out of energy, will, focus?

Or I get angry, sad, frustrated, etc.?

Or I get so depressed I can't function?

All of these are ancient, natural responses to stresses caused by change. Thousands of years ago, our ancient ancestors had to watch what they did very carefully. Trusting people, you did not know might result in you being beat and having your provisions stolen.

Today, there is not nearly the chance of that happening, but we've all had this possibility etched into our minds and it is very hard to get those thoughts, behaviors and beliefs about what is in our own best interest out of our heads. Our behavior and the personality that behavior produces, more often than not, is counterproductive, and quite of self-destructive, in today's world.

Change is critical for our own health, safety, happiness, and sense of self worth. But change is going against our very own human nature and millennia of survival "instincts," that have worked in a hostile and extremely dangerous world. The vast majority of these behaviors now cause far more stress than they ever had the potential to relieve. Mankind needs, desperately needs, a new mindset which focuses on cooperation and creating a positive sense of community. But how do we cast off the old and adapt, integrate, and become a whole way of looking at our world? Quite honestly, if it was easy to create and adopt a new mindset, our own imbedded person belief system would probably derail our efforts more quickly than anyone would give those old behavioral instincts credit to.

Before we can change, we must know what characteristics about ourselves, we dislike most! Perhaps it's that you get frustrated too easily! (It takes too long, or I don't have enough TIME to get everything done.) Or that you are too concerned about what others think about you! (PEOPLE) Maybe, you are too desirous of what other people seem to have! Some people feel like they will never have as much as others have! Or perhaps jealousy burns you to your core. (THINGS)When we look at what creates discontentment the most, we usually realize that one of these three things are at fault:

People (including myself), places (and all the "stuff associated with those places) and time.

How can we change?

Fortunately, the research is very clear and very decisive. Perfect practice produces perfect OUTCOMES! Here are the steps that work if you make a 100% commitment to using the 4 times per day for a minimum of 21 days without fail and that you are honest about recording your daily results without any kind of evaluative comments. In your daily recording of your results, note the following:

1. what are the strongest emotions you feel at the end of your 4th session of the day?

2. How do you feel physically?

3. How well rested do you feel?

4. What changes in your life have you observed?

Now do these things:

1. Identify the critical emotions and/or human qualities that you want as the key characteristics of your life? Remember, respect, happiness, peace, joy, satisfaction, love, etc. based on what others do, depends upon their ability to do what you want them to do! How successful has that been in the past? No matter how hard we try, we

can never control how others behave. So let's identify emotions, characteristics, and/or personality traits that will create a more peaceful life and have a greater chance for us to produce a positive result for our life. Enter these emotions, characteristics, and personality traits below in the appropriate section.

2. Perfecting these new, more positive and healthy attitudes, requires experiences that allow us to practice under a variety of conditions. What do you see as circumstances and/or situations you've found to be challenging in the past? These past circumstances and/or situations, in your previous life would have served as a means by which you would give up on the new characteristics or personality traits. Your established brain and established body would work to make your life miserable until you did, indeed, return to your old ways. Enter one or two of these experiences in the appropriate section below.

3. The three layers approach to exchanging one's old self for a new and better self! First we must clearly think about, imagine if you will, how we will engage with our world as we implement our new qualities and characteristics. Next, our old self would react to these changes by telling you that what you are doing is dangerous. You'll get hurt or sick or taken advantage of. Remember these are excuses that the world is making to keep you from changing. Be

still, quiet, and allow God to work in your life. Be steadfast in your prayer and meditation.

Remember, there are millions of people trying to make profound changes in their lives. There are 8 billion people on our planet. So, you are in the less than 10% who are even making a serious attempt. Furthermore there are less than 1 million people who really will make the complete transformation, which is to say that less than .2% of us will succeed. Should you complete the journey, please share your success, you may be amazed at the true benefits of sharing.

Is there a biblical basis for this! Absolutely! Look at these biblical heroes who did so!

And he (Jesus) told them a parable to show that they must always pray and not be discouraged, saying, "There was a certain judge in a certain town who did not fear God and did not respect people. And there was a widow in that town, and she kept coming to him, saying, 'Grant me justice against my adversary!' And he was not willing for a time, but after these things he said to himself, 'Even if I do not fear God or respect people, yet because this widow is causing trouble for me, I will grant her justice, so that she does not wear me down in the end by her coming back!'" And the Lord said, "Listen to what the unrighteous judge is saying! And will not God surely see to it that justice is done to his chosen ones who cry out to him day and night, and will he delay toward them? I tell you that he will see to it that justice is done for them soon! Nevertheless, when the Son of Man comes, then will he find faith on earth?" Luke 18:1-8 Everyday, that Judge, who heard the pleading of the widow, day after day, changed his heart. She made him think, and he changed his response as a result.

"So I say to you, ask, and it will be given to you; seek, and you will find; knock, and it will be opened to you. For everyone who asks receives, and he who seeks finds, and to him who knocks it will be opened.

"If a son asks for bread from any father among you, will he give him a stone? Or if he asks for a fish, will he give him a serpent instead of a fish? Or if he asks for an egg, will he offer him a scorpion?

"If you then, being evil, know how to give good gifts to your children, how much more will your heavenly Father give the Holy Spirit to those who ask Him!" Luke 11:9-13

"Give ear to my words, O LORD, consider my meditation. Give heed to the voice of my cry, my King and my God, for to You I will pray" (Psalm 5:1-2).

"For the LORD does not see as man sees, for man looks at the outward appearance, but the LORD looks at the heart" (1 Samuel 16:7).

Heavenly Creator of all that exists, give me the strength I need to truly let go. Help me pray unceasingly, from my heart. I know this only comes when I can quiet the noise, open my heart, and merge my spirit with yours. I realize that this can only happen is I am as persistent at the widow. Not because You are resistant because I resist and have too little faith. My persistence is not about your willingness but my lack of serious devotion to you. Lead towards your everlasting love! Amen

Day 28

A Devotional for Understanding and Acceptance

Let's see if we can find a way to apply these principles to our self improvement and our faith!

Why is it that people who play music, or play a sport such baseball, or golf, or soccer believe that rehearsals/practice sessions are essential to success, but people who "work" for a living believe practice sessions/rehearsals are a waste of time and money? Maybe, just maybe, every business, every classroom, every government employee, needs to stop working and start playing! If they all stopped working and started playing at these other careers, they'd see that the best way to do their job well is to rehearse how they're hoping to perform the tasks laid before them!

So, does mental rehearsal really work? You be the judge! Here's an message I wrote for the Western Michigan Women's Basketball Team On Mental Rehearsal and its impact on Athletic Endeavors.

Basketball Edition

How do we mentally rehearse? It is a detailed type of Visualization. It captures "The Power of a Movie Theater you can create in your own mind.

Introduction

You don't need to touch a basketball to improve your game. Simply by using your mind to practice, you can get tangible results. Visualization is the psychological practice of rehearsing and imagining yourself playing successfully as if it were a movie.

The Zone

Have you ever witnessed a game where someone was "in the zone"? Maybe you've had a similar experience in a game where you were clicking on all cylinders. Michael Jordan often commented that when he was in the zone, it happened without thought. He could often remain in the zone for several minutes, but as soon as he started thinking about what he was doing, WHAM!!!! He was no longer in the zone! The worst thing an athlete can do is question their ability by thinking about what they need to do. Let your muscle memory take over, and Keep your conscious thinking out of your game!

Were you thinking about how to shoot? Were you remembering to bend your knees, get your elbow at a 90 degree angle under the ball, keep your fingers spread out, and hold your follow through? Probably not. It's muscle memory! Keep your conscious thinking out of your game!

When you ask someone who's experienced being in the zone what they were thinking about, the answer is usually "nothing" or "I wasn't thinking". They are often described as "playing out of their mind" or being "unconscious". Evidently, some part of the mind is not active. Why? Someone in the zone is said to be "feeling it" (getting emotionally connected to the process rather than thinking about the process) therefore the player is not thinking it or remembering instructions- because images are more powerful than words and showing is better than telling. Their mind is focused on the mental image of the desired outcome. It's the art of relaxed concentration through visualization. **Keep your conscious thinking out of your game!**

Free Throw Experiment

In the 1950's at the University of Chicago, Dr. Biasiotto conducted a study on how effective visualization could be in enhancing performance- specifically for basketball players. The players were split into 3 groups. Over the course of a month, the first group was told to spend an hour a day practicing free throws. The second group was told to just visualize themselves making free throws every day. The third group was told to do nothing.

The third group saw no improvements. However, the second group shot 23% better, and the first group shot 24% better. The second group improved their free throw shooting percentage without touching a basketball. They were only 1 percentage point below those who worked on it every day for an hour. Now, imagine how much improvement would take place if a player used visualization in addition to diligent practice.

So, who are the great basket ball players that used mental rehearsal (I use the term mental rehearsal because the most commonly used term is Visualization, and that tends to result in failure to understand that rehearsal requires more than just seeing, it expects some type of performing based on a best practice which uses key mechanics and habits to achieve a desired outcome.

Here are 2 NBA superstars that utilized mental rehearsal: Michael Jordan and Kobe Bryant.

Based on the research cited, here's my training program for becoming an excellent free throw shooter! I had and will continue to have my basketball players do both the daily practice using all the proper mechanics and visualizing themselves using the proper form & making a mental movie of me (each player is their own me/my), making 100 straight free throws. The main thing is: **Keep your conscious thinking out of your game!**

For the active practice activity, I put tape on the floor at 4 places: 1st—2 feet in front of the free throw line, 2nd—4 feet up, 3rd—6 feet, and 4th—8 feet up. Each player must make 20 shots from each tape mark and then 30 from the Free Throw Line: Here's how the process for these free throws. At the first line (closest to the basket) the player must make 15 shots and then make 5 blindfolded! All blindfold shots are done as follows: as with the shots without the blindfold, the shooter followers their own routine, and then will say to their FT partner, blindfold and the partner will move the blindfold over their FT partner's eyes. Then the shooter makes their shot. This repeated until the shooter has made 5! This repeated at all the tape lines, then at the free throw line if the shooter makes 30 without a miss, the shooter is finished with the drill. If there is a miss, the shooter must attempt a blindfold shot for every missed free throw of the 30 attempts.

Keep your conscious thinking out of your game!

Using this training program I saw dramatic improvements in every player I coached!

Every sport has examples of mental practice, visualization, or creating images from memory of successful actions.

In baseball, how about these:

Sandy Koufax, Derek Jeter, Aaron Judge, Hank Aaron, Bruce Souter, Roberto Clemente:

Each of these super stars will tell you, over and over and over again; **<u>Keep your conscious thinking out of your game! And so will these;</u>**

◦ Distance Runner—Steve Prefontaine,

◦ Golf superstar, Tiger Woods,

◦ Tennis Superstars—Serena Williams and Sister Venus Williams, Raphael Nadal,

◦ European Football: Beckham

◦ Olympic Decathlon: Bob Mathias, Ashton Eaton, and Dan O'Brien.

Now to him who is able to do immeasurably more than all we ask or imagine, according to his power that is at work within us, to him be glory in the church and in Christ Jesus throughout all generations, for ever and ever! Amen. Ephesians 3:20-21

Day 29

A Devotional for Understanding and Acceptance

Why are we here?

I apologize for the long devotional post yesterday. I've been trying make these posts very practical and those were words created for my athlete grandchildren and the young adults on the teams I've been working with!

Today's devotional, is much shorter.

Why do we get side tracked in our Faith Journey?

Jesus stayed focused, and never misunderstood why he was here. We, these newest children of God, have a hard time accepting that the battle is already won! There is nothing you can do to help!

"It is finished!" John 19:30

This is the last idea shared by Jesus. Most biblical scholars believe what Jesus meant by this was, everything he came to do, his purpose, was completed. He died so that we might realize that death was not a curse, it was not the end but a gateway to a new better life and spiritual connection to our Creator. But, WE, The People, just won't accept, we want to do it! We have been given a place at the table and a room in the House of "GREATEST PARENT OF ALL TIME," The Living Lord of Life!

On the cross he shared love and forgave his executioners, and the thieves who were crucified with him. We must be more about forgiveness than condemnation. If we cannot find it within ourselves, we will destroy everything that God Created. For Jesus did his part, now we must do ours. Stop trying to fix things and your efforts you can never do better than God, who truly wants us to Love not hate!

Jesus told us he did not come to abolish the Laws and the Prophesies, but to fulfill them. Jesus defied the rules of the time! Rather than throw stones at an adulterous woman, he was merciful. This definitely told us laws are good for the unfaithful but the greatest gift of all is always love! Jesus told us that the scriptures that ruled the people of ancient Israel, were not as important as Love: Love of God and Love for one another! Jesus is telling us all, show me a law or prophecy, and I will show Love that makes that Law or Prophecy unnecessary.

Heavenly Creator of all People, all living creatures, every rock, metal, gas, liquid, idea, and everything beyond and in between, Thank you for your Unconditional Live. Help me realize, that If I work, very, very hard to get everything I think I need to be worthy of a seat close to you at the Eternal Dining Table, if in that process,

I am push others aside and rejecting the very people (adulterers, foreigners, ethnically diverse, people who just are too different) that Jesus loves, I move myself to the end of the line. As far away from my Creator as possible! Help be open, affirming, accepting of everything God Created. It has never been my or anyone else's place, only God's, the First Earth Born Child of God's, and the Holy Spirit's place to say where each person's place is in heaven. Help us all understand that the words you've inspired great people of the past to write so that we can have guidance, are just that, a guide. Amen

Day 30

A Devotional for Understanding and Acceptance

According to Dr. Steve Sisler, an Axiologist, and an expert on human behavior (Axiology is the study of human values development and their impact on behavior) there are 4 main human emotions. In his book, The Four People Types, he discusses these 4 key emotions:

Mad (Angry), Glad (Happy), Sad (Depressed) and Scared. According to Steve Sisler, any other emotion we can think of could be considered to be related to one of these.

When we read the Gospels, we see many references to a full line of what could be considered emotions associated with Glad! Here are just a few of those!

"These things have I spoken to you, that My joy may remain in you, and that your joy may be full." John 15:11

Until now you have asked nothing in my name. Ask, and you will receive, that your joy may be full. John 16:24

His master said to him, "Well done, good and faithful servant. You have been faithful over a little; I will set you over much. Enter into the joy of your master." Matthew 25:21

Great Creator God, thank you for wanting us all to be joyful, glad, happy, and have the opportunity to bask in your light and love. Please help us overcome our fears, set aside our anger, and bring our sadness into the light and change our tears of sadness into love drenched happiness. We know we are blessed and praise you for all that you have created and allow us to manage. I pray that more and more of us will realize that you do not create so that we can waste. It is our responsibility to care for all of creation and I pray that more and more Christians will join in our quest to preserve your marvelous creation! Amen

Day 31

A Devotional for Understanding and Acceptance

Can anyone ever provide an unbiassed set of facts?

Have you ever noticed that 5 different people can experience the same event in 5 different ways. Have you also noticed that each of those observers might think that each of the other 4 people are either completely wrong or are being very deceitful. The question: is it possible that experience of reality can be different based on who is observing a given situation? Furthermore, is it possible for different people, observing the same circumstances and coming to a different conclusion, to all be correct and accurate in their interpretation of the situation? In fact, you might have a different take on events as a 20-year-old, than you would as a 40 year old or a 60 year old.

Whenever I hear someone say this is the Truth, the whole Truth, and nothing but the Truth; my response is always, "your truth, based on your perspective, which is based on your life experiences, and the biases those experiences have created. No interpretation of what we observe is ever uninfluenced by the way we view our world. And our view, whether you want to admit or not, is always full of our own special biases and prejudices.

Don't get me wrong, not everyone who has a differing opinion has that different notion based on an honest, although biased view! We are, at times, confronted by intentionally contrary individuals. There are definitely, people who will say anything, and twist a well intentioned person's most vulnerable emotions towards a state of incredible fear.

Throughout the centuries, there has never been a lack of evil, yet influential men, who have utilized the fear of vulnerable people to create political movements that, at first suggest and later emphatically state that specific ideas and people are responsible for the ills that our world faces. I will not point out any of the scapegoats that have fueled so many atrocities over the centuries. I am quite sure you are aware of many, and you may even be from one of these groups yourself. However, I am just as positive that there are some you never realized were used as scapegoats by others!

After this I looked, and behold, a great multitude that no one could number, from every nation, from all tribes and peoples and languages, standing before the throne and before the Lamb, clothed in white robes, with palm branches in their hands. Revelations 7:9

But if you show partiality, you are committing sin and are convicted by the law as transgressors. James 2:9

So, Peter opened his mouth and said: "Truly I understand that God shows no partiality," Acts 10:34

Gracious Lord: let us never forget the innocent people who throughout the ages have been enslaved, tortured, murdered, and a used for all manners of excuses as scapegoats to free us and others from accepting the responsibility of our own mistakes and weaknesses.

There can be no better prayer than the prayer attributed to St. Francis

Lord, make me an instrument of your peace where there is hatred, let me sow love where there is injury, pardon where there is doubt, faith where there is despair, hope where there is darkness, light where there is sadness, joy. O divine Master, grant that I may not so much seek to be consoled as to console to be understood as to understand to be loved as to love.

For it is in giving that we receive, it is in pardoning that we are pardoned, and it is in dying that we are born to eternal life Amen.

Day 32

A Devotional for Understanding and Acceptance

The question is not, Who is God? The real question is: What is God?

Because humans look like they do, we have a tendency to see God in human terms with a human likeness. In Genesis, the author states that humans were made in God's image, so those who dared to take that notion verbatim, have an idea that God must be a very old human sitting on clouds way up in the sky. But, when all of this was created, including living things, there was an order and a sequence.

In the beginning God created the heavens and the earth. Now the earth was formless and empty, darkness was over the surface of the deep, and the **Spirit** of God was hovering over the waters.

And God said, "Let there be light," and there was light.

God saw that the light was good, and he separated the light from the darkness. God called the light "day," and the darkness he called "night." And there was evening, and there was morning—the first day." Genesis 1:1-5 The Bold type and underlining was placed by me to emphasize that it was the Spirit that made The

Great I am different from Zeus, or Apollo, RAH, or any of the other deities worshipped by members of other cultures. The One true God was separated from humanity by existing in a Spiritual form. Elohim is the Hebrew word used to refer to a deity, which is how we might refer to Roman, Greek or Hindu gods. Elohim is used in the original Hebrew Bible (Pentateuch or Torah) primarily to speak of the creator God. For example, in Genesis 1:1 it says, "In the beginning Elohim created the heavens and the earth". It could be said that The One True Deity Created the Heavens and the Earth and all that exists!

Moses said to God, "Suppose I go to the Israelites and say to them, 'The God of your fathers has sent me to you,' and they ask me, 'What is his name?' Then what shall I tell them?" God said to Moses, "I AM WHO I AM. This is what you are to say to the Israelites: 'I AM has sent me to you.'" Exodus 3:13-14

I AM, is derived from the verb "to be." God just "is." God self-existed, exists and will always exist eternally. God has no beginning and no end. God wasn't created, wasn't formed, and God is unlike anything we can see, explain or imagine. Put it another way, God answers Moses, "I am everything, I own it all, I created everything, I give life, I sustain life, I sustain everything, I AM!" How do you name that or Him!?

The Hebrew word for "I am" is pronounced Eh-Yeh. However, the Hebrew people would not say this name or write it in full because they felt as mere mortals, human beings should not say His name (although that is not instructed in the Bible). Thus, instead of writing or saying Eh-Yeh, they wrote the four letters YHWH (known as the tetragrammaton) to represent His name. YHWH is not pronounceable because the vowels have been removed, so Yahweh, is how they eventually began pronouncing YHWH. However, Yahweh too, was considered too holy to say, so Adonai is what the Jewish people called Him. Adonai is the Hebrew word for Lord, someone who was over another person, like a master.

I have been asked: for those who affirm God's pre-eminent state, and accept his offer of grace, will we know our friends and loved ones in the afterlife? If we read the Bible carefully, we discover that Jesus describes the afterlife with great clarity.

"Let not your hearts be troubled. Believe in God; believe also in me. In my Father's house are many rooms. If it were not so, would I have told you that I go to prepare a place for you? And if I go and prepare a place for you, I will come again and will take you to myself, that where I am you may be also. And you know the way to where I am going." John 14:1-4

"For when they rise from the dead, they neither marry, nor are given in marriage, but are like angels in heaven. Mark 12:25

for neither can they die anymore, for they are like angels, and are sons of God, being sons of the resurrection. Luke 20:36

Amazing Creator of all that is known and unknown. We realize that we are not these earthly bodies in which our spiritual beings presently find shelter. In that day, when our spirits are set free, we will know that we are connected to the essence of life for every soul that had ever lived. We thank you for your infinite wisdom and your extraordinary plan for each and every human being. Help us to discover that our mission, whether we like it or not, is to lead as many to you as we possibly can. We also know this is best done with the loving attitude that draws people to the better spiritual life that is made available by you to everyone. Help us all accept this gift with gratitude and a heart that reflects your abundance and love. Amen

Day 33

A Devotional for Understanding and Acceptance

Why am I so uncomfortable?

Jesus did not try to make us feel comfortable! For Jesus, and our Great Creator, physical comfort was never the Goal. If it was, Jesus would not have spent 40 days in the desert ("And Jesus, full of the Holy Spirit, returned from the Jordan, and was led by the Spirit for forty days in the wilderness, tempted by the devil. And he ate nothing in those days; and when they were ended, he was hungry" Luke, Chapter 4, verses 1-2). creating the perfect connection to the Spirit of the Living God!

If comfort was God's Goal for us, there would never have been a need for the Hebrew Nation to wander through the desert after leaving Egypt. (And the Lord added, that same generation of those that murmured will wander in the wilderness "According to the number of the days in which you spied out the land, 40 days, for each day you shall bear your guilt with one year, namely 40 years" Numbers 14:34 If comfort was truly the Goal, why allow life at all?

As each of us makes our own path through life, we have the opportunity to create the opportunity for as many people, from as many different cultures, races, genders, religions, and political philosophies as possible; or we can choose to create comfort for ourselves at the expense of many of those same people!

Discomfort happens whenever we must face change. Change is required if we are ever going to grow. Whether that growth is intellectual, physical, emotional, or spiritual; as we navigate those changes, we are bound to deal with some discomfort. Because we do not agree with an idea, doesn't make that idea something we should not explore. In the fall of 1971, as I was completing my degree requirements for my bachelor's degree. I needed to 2 additional history courses, 1 each of the first two trimesters to qualify for my degree. I wanted to really experience two of the best history professors at my College. In the fall, I registered for a class in African History and for the winter session I registered for a course in African-American History. Both of the classes challenged this Norther European descended, American Suburban young man. I am so incredibly glad I had that experience. I have the rich history of Africa, and what happened to many Africans as they were brought to North America in conditions worse than were cattle!

This knowledge conditioned my beliefs in a way that helped me truly understand why The Apostle Paul was so adamant that God does not play favorites. And Jesus told us that if Ed subjugate people, placing ourselves above them? Those first now, will be last, while those who are put in last position now, will be first!

Dear Creator, my love for all you created is only second in my eyes to to my love and devotion to you. Please remind every single person, every single day, that if you want to be in the highest order among the angels in heaven, you must be willing to jet everyone else go first in everything you do! AMEN!

Day 34

A Devotional for Understanding and Acceptance

When we were growing up, did we like the nice people and dislike the bullies?

If we really think about it, none of us really liked and respected bullies. I've known many bullies over the last 70 years, and most of them didn't like bullies. In fact, the vast majority of bullies, think they've been bullied so they have a right to fight for what they believe is due them! Once we can get a Bully to describe what they think is bullying behavior, and then have them describe their own behavior, we often find they will use subtle things to differentiate their behavior from bullies and justify their own behavior while condemning others who they attribute bullying behavior to. When a bully convinces masses of people that he or she is only helping to level the playing field, they are laying the foundation for behavior that just might be considered totalitarian or even Dictatorial. This, they insist is because "A, B, and/or C" have so altered the ground that is the foundation for that playing field that it will always end up tipping in their favor. Without an intervention, those who have the power today, may be in such a disadvantaged position in the future that they and their ancestors may never be able to recover their lost positions of "Leadership."

This is not just a liberal red herring regarding current political maneuvers by conservative politicians. Neither is it a red herring launched by conservative politicians trying to blame our current issues on the overreaching actions perpetrated by the liberals who've been in power. This is being introduced to suggest that it's not about liberalism or conservatism. It is about the extreme positions held by "bullies" who will use the politics of division and hatred to make sure they get what they've determined they are entitled to! During the past few decades, the divisive mantra has been "those people who want to rewrite history!" For several decades prior, the mantra was "those who were too comfy and beholding to the ruling class; The bourgeoisie! It really doesn't matter to a Hitler or a Stalin, the key is not the others; the key is Hitler himself or Stalin himself. Or Castro himself. Or Pol Pot. Or the leaders of the KKK. Or King Herod. Or ————: you fill in the blank!

They've all had their day in the limelight! They will be the last to be accepted at the throne of our savior! Those who were subjugated by them will be moved far ahead! Those who do the bidding of these manipulators, will find their place as well. And the Prince of Peace, Emmanuel, God with us, will ask us: How did you receive and care for me when I was homeless, sick, unjustly imprisoned, and beaten and bloodied.

"Then the King will say to those on his right, 'Come, you who are blessed by my Father, inherit the kingdom prepared for you from the foundation of the world. For I was hungry and you gave me food, I was thirsty and you gave me drink, I was a stranger and you welcomed me, I was naked and you clothed me, I was sick and you visited me, I was in prison and you came to me.' Then the righteous will answer him, saying, 'Lord, when did we see you hungry and feed you, or thirsty and give you drink? And when did we see you a stranger and welcome you, or naked and clothe you?" Matthew: 24:34-40

"I For I was hungry, and you gave me nothing to eat, I was thirsty, and you gave me nothing to drink, I was a stranger, and you did not invite me in, I needed clothes and you did not clothe me, I was sick and in prison and you did not look after me.' They also will answer, 'Lord, when did we see you hungry or thirsty or a stranger or needing clothes or sick or in prison, and did not help you?'

He will reply, 'Truly I tell you, whatever you did not do for one of the least of these, you did not do for me." Matthew 24: 41-45.

Dear Lord of Host, Savior God:

Please remind me with your continuous presence in my heart, to always be open and welcoming to the least of these, my brothers and sisters who are truly in need, that how I treat them is how I am continuously treating the Christ. Help live my life as a good and faithful servant as described in Matthew 24: vs 34-40. Not so much that we get to move up a few spaces in line but because our kindness and generosity just might help a few of our bothers and sisters realize that this line is not just me and my Christian's in church, but this line is open and welcoming for anyone who is open, accepting, and one who loves God. AMEN

Day 35

A Devotional for Understanding and Acceptance

Why am I hurting so badly?

I can recall so clearly the day my sister passed. I knew something was really wrong. My Dad called us, and he never called. My mom was the communicator in our family. My sister's life was tumultuous. The youngest of 4 kids, only girl, and she never really felt like she truly fit in. Alison, or as my brother Bert liked to call her: Nosila. My dad was from a different era. A whole other space-Time continuum it seems. He didn't realize that what he thought we harmless little jokes and nicknames could be so hurtful. Example, my sister he called "my little round girl! As a little 3 and 4 year old, she was not terribly upset with our dad, but as she starred kindergarten, and the in to 1st grade the sting became very real. Alison tried for several years to find her identity, to figure out who and what she was meant to be.

As a 1st grader, she wanted to be like the boys. Bert chipped in, you can't play baseball, you can't even slide into second base. Alison, remarked I can too, and ran across the living room and slid into the coffee table, twisting her leg into a very weird shape. She let out an ear piercing scream, whimpered, and passed out. Our Mom and Dad cam running to the living room, yelled at we three boys, "What the h*** happened. My mom scooped Alison up in her arms, which brought Alison to a blood curdling scream level of pain, and as my was obviously mad, he told our older brother Mark, you're in charge until we get back. They put Alison in the back seat, mom sat next Alison and put Alison's head on her lap and as my dad drove out of side he yelled tell the Taylor's (our next door neighbors) what happened. We'll be back as soon as we can. Alison had a spiral fracture of her left femur. It was the last attempt, she ever made to try to compete with anyone in any athletic endeavor.

What we do, how we do it, and why we do it? All of this matters. How often do we do things and not even think about it? Too much of our lives are conducted in an nearly unconscious state. If confronted about the impact of our actions too many of us want those we've harmed to just, " Get over it!" It is time for all of us to "WAKE UP!" We can't allow any more disasters to be created by the sleep walking masses. Add to these negligence created horrors, the intentional chaos created by some truly misguided people and the damage just explodes in scope and intensity.

The long term consequences of poorly planned actions, those that defy logic and result in far reaching damage were discussed in the Old Testament:

I lavish unfailing love to a thousand generations. I forgive iniquity, rebellion, and sin. But I do not excuse the guilty. I lay the sins of the parents up on their children and grandchildren; the entire family is affected — even children in the third and fourth generations. Exodus 34:7 This actually not an act of condemnation, but truly a description of the calamity we bring on ourselves.

Today I have given you the choice between life and death, between blessings and curses. Now I call on heaven and earth to witness the choice you make. Oh, that you would choose life, so that you and your descendants might live!

Deuteronomy 30:19

Thank you Dear God, forgiving us a choice as to how we will live our lives. Let us Awake, and be fully aware of what we are doing and the impact that has on not just ourselves, but others, as well. Let us decide to Choose life, awaken our minds, hearts, bodies, and souls, so that we are completely aware of all we do! Please help us become completely, fully alive. AMEN

Day 36

A Devotional for Understanding and Acceptance

What are you hiding and why are you hiding it?

"Can a man hide himself in hiding places So I do not see him?" declares the Lord. Do I not fill the heavens and the earth?" declares the Lord. Jeremiah 23:24

"For nothing is hidden that will not become evident, nor anything secret that will not be known and come to light." Luke 8:17

I know that I have tried to keep a few (maybe more than a few) things secret. Why have I done that? I know my reason has always been fear. I've been afraid that some may use certain things against me, if they knew those things about me. I've also been afraid that if certain other things came to light, some people I care very much about, might be hurt. However, as the years have gone by, most of the information gets out any way. And you know what, I've discovered that most people are very forgiving and hardly ever have a reaction that even comes close to what fearful imagination conjured up. And, as far as anyone using information about me to make life difficult, those who would try to do so don't need the truth about me to make life difficult. There have been many times when those who wish I would fail, never were too concerned about what they've said was true or not. Their goal was to put me in my place and when someone has that attitude and goal, the best defense is always transparency!

We see when so much deceit and outright fabrications of stories, we lose faith in our leaders, our friends, our coworkers, and too often we start to doubt people we rely on. Doctors, lawyers, teachers, school board members, small town mayors, police, EMTs, and even our neighbors seem to not really care enough. My advice is, don't let anyone else poison your attitude about we rely on for having a more positive and meaningful life. Give people the benefit of the doubt and see if they have more integrity than the detractors give them credit for.

So now faith, hope, and love abide, these three; but the greatest of these is love. 1Corinthians 13:13

So we have come to know and to believe the love that God has for us. God is love, and whoever abides in love abides in God, and God abides in him.

1John 4:16

Heavenly Gracious God, help each of your flock know your love, caring and guidance. Let us be open, transparent, accepting and a generous in the light of the marvelous gift you have given us. Lead us away from our hiding places and reveal the good you have waiting for each of us. You alone know the truth about each of us and your offer of salvation still lies ahead of us. We are forgiven! Hallelujah AMEN!

Day 37

A Devotional for Understanding and Acceptance

Is there a way that we can be closer to God?

I often feel as if I am just going through the motions. My faith waivers, I feel awful for doubting, and then I realize that Jesus warned us of thinking that we are this human body. Psychologists have named this intellectual condition as our Ego. Our Ego is not real, it is only our perception of who we are and what we think we need in order for us to survive. In order for us to experience the presence of God in our lives, we must do as Jesus has taught us all. We must live a life focused on connecting to the extraordinary love that can only come from our Amazing Gracious God! As long as the desire to be who we think we are is stronger than our desire to be what the Spirit of the living God sees us as, there will be what appears to be a an insurmountable obstacle blocking our path.

As Billy Graham taught to those would listen, Remember, we get to know a person by spending time together. All that we know about God is found in the Bible. The Holy Spirit is our Teacher as we read the Bible. Through His living Word, He speaks to us; and through prayer, we speak to Him. It is a dialogue.

Billy Graham was quite consistent with his message: "We need to spend from 30 minutes to 60 minutes at the start of the day. I like to walk and pray after I have spent time in reading and meditation in the Word. When finished, I don't say, 'Goodbye, Lord. I'll see you tomorrow.' Rather, I say, 'Lord, let's go. What exciting things are going to happen in my life today?' I find myself communing with God many times during the day."

We cannot know all there is to know about God, but we can enjoy His presence every waking moment of the rest of our lives. This is the abiding relationship. Paul also taught us that God said, "Never will I leave you; never will I forsake you" (Hebrews 13:5). Be in a constant, ongoing relationship with the Creator. And you might discover that peace that is beyond all understanding, and sense that we all matter.

Heavenly Creator God, help me know you and your powerful presence in my life. Let me accept that as I look at the world and my fellow humans, that I can see them and yet Cannot physically see myself, yet I too often think everyone should be more concerned with me and my place in the world, than I ever show to them. Forgive me for my arrogance and short sightedness. I pray that we might all discover a deeper, more loving connection with you. Thank you, Gracious God. Let us all see that your glory is truly the manifestation of the gentlest, caring, amazing, LOVE Ever known. Again, I say Hallelujah AMEN!

Day 38

A Devotional for Understanding and Acceptance

Why did Jesus have such a strong message about how we should think about children and their approach to what they believe?

"When the sun goes down, and the moon comes up, everybody goes night-night. Mommy goes night-night, daddy goes night-night." This was a song, sung by a 3-year-old to his parents, as he lay down to sleep one night. It's amazing what thoughts stay in our heads for such a long time. I remember when I was 7 or 8, reading a few versus from a children's Bible about Jesus ascending into heaven. While imagining that event, I, a child who had not yet attended a church service, experienced a moment of amazing clarity that God was real and it made my heart feel warm, my eyes see a shining, glorious light, and gave me a sense of safety, that I continue to pray for, for all people.

Why did Jesus say, "Let the children come to me; do not hinder them, for to such belongs the kingdom of God. Truly, I say to you, whoever does not receive the kingdom of God like a child shall not enter it" Mark 10:14-15.

Children, at least most of them, have very open minds and truly believe anything is possible. These children lack the limitations in their thinking that older people often have. We frequently refer to the belief that some things just aren't possible, as being jaded! The term jaded refers to being worn down by ideas that never produced the outcomes you expected. Children approach their relationship with God full of hope and positive expectation.

The world sometimes misunderstands the idea of childlike faith, thinking that Christians are childlike because they believe in myths and fairytales. But this is not the Bible's meaning when it compares us to children. Instead, childlike faith is a metaphor for trust, dependence and love, and an encouragement to ask for what we need. "If you, then, though you are evil, know how to give good gifts to your children, how much more will your Father in heaven give good gifts to those who ask him! Matthew: 7:11

Lord Jesus, my redeemer and Savior, we pray that you will help us regain that unjaded, trusting faith that stems from our belief that God, the magnificent Creator truly does have the desire and power and will to assist us in our journey through this world. We do realize that what we experience in this life is influenced by how we interpret what happens. The choices we make about what event outcomes mean, can bind us to a negative world or free us from that bondage. Help us choose Joyfulness and Happy times. Let us remember that the Apostle Paul clearly directed us all, over and over in his letters to the early the church leaders:

Rejoice in hope. . . . Rejoice with those who rejoice" Romans 12:12-15. "Finally, brothers, rejoice" 2 Corinthians 13:1. "Rejoice always" 1 Thessalonians. "Be glad and rejoice with me" Philippians 2:18. "Rejoice in the Lord" Philippians 3:1. "Rejoice in the Lord always; again I will say, rejoice" Philippians 4:4. AMEN

Day 39

A Devotional for Understanding and Acceptance

How can we explain, in as kind of a way possible, that expecting a child of yours to exceed your achievements will take more dedication, focus, and learning/training than they were willing to devote to that same task?

Living vicariously through the success of your children has truly become the Great American Past-Time! Just a little over a century ago, the American dream was for the Children in a family to carry on the family tradition. If Dad worked in the mines, or the steel plant, or farmed, or were doctors, lawyers, teachers, soldiers, or what have you, the boys in that family were expected to work in the same arena. The entire notion of becoming a professional musician, athlete, or actor was not just frowned upon, but were discouraged as a total waste of time. In fact, in 1919, the average salary of a professional baseball player was $2,400 a year. 40 years later, in 1959, the average salary was $16, 997 a year. The average household income in 1919 was approximately $3,250. By 1929, it had grown to $6,132, but dropped to $4,880 in 1930, and dropped to $1,850. Of course, this was the heart of the Great Depression. By 1950, it had grown back to $3,400 and by 1959 it was $5,950.

So, by 1959, becoming a Major League Baseball player had definite financial rewards. It continued to become more lucrative with each succeeding year so that today, the best players are most likely in the game.

In the early years of professional baseball, the financial rewards were not what they are today. So, quite honestly, because of the incentives today, the competition for the positions, even at the lowest level of college and minor league baseball, is more heated than ever before. So, if a youth sports participant desires to put in the training effort to possibly achieve greatness, the odds are strongly against them. The key is what will it take to get there and then answer this, very important question. Are you truly ready, willing, and able to devote the time, energy, finances, and sense of self-importance to get the job done. It is a long, straight, and very narrow road to travel. If you are the parent or parents of a youth athlete, know that your life and sense of achievement, does not, has not, and never will change based on how well, how far, or how much your children achieve.

"Do everything without grumbling and arguing so that you may be blameless and pure, innocent children of God surrounded by people who are crooked and corrupt. Among these people you shine like stars in the world." Philippians 2:14-15

And Jesus was very clear about the path to achieving the truly great life. Enter through the narrow gate. For wide is the gate and broad is the road that leads to destruction, and many enter through it. But small is the gate and narrow the road that leads to life, and only a few find it. Matthew 7:13-14

Lord of Life, thank you for pointing out the most productive, although incredibly narrow and difficult path to the best life possible. Help us understand the dedication required, the personal changes we must make, and though we don't want to discourage genuine efforts to rise to the occasion, we do want to make sure that everyone's aware of the need to make these efforts for the purest of reasons. Please, great redeemer, help us recognize the broad roadway that is filled with destructive desires and false promises. Help us all realize that even the most talented achievers we're not born that way. It requires dedication, focus, and the channeling of needed resources to help us stay on that narrow, but productive path. Create is us a clean and pure heart Oh Marvelous Creator, generate that right spirit so that we will always be fulfilling your will as we move forward. AMEN

Day 40

A Devotional for Understanding and Acceptance

How do we keep from losing our faith among so many faithless people?

Here are 6 excellent suggestions from some magnificent Christian people with powerful faith.

1. Regularly Examine Your Faith.

2. Find Inspiration in Biblical Figures.

3. Take Solace in Prayer.

4. Connect with a Faith-Based Community.

5. Do Good in the World.

6. Show Compassion.

Today we will look at the first of these and then over the next 5 days, we'll look more closely at the next 5.

Regularly Examine Your Faith. Introspection is essential. Take time to realize that what you believe the world is doing to you is an illusion. How you respond to the events in your life will determine how you feel about those events. As long as you play the victim in each of the negative outcome events, rather than trying to learn from those events, you will suffer from anger, sadness, and fear. When we shift to a learning mindset, we open the doors to joy, happiness, and a sense of hope for the future.

Examine yourselves to see whether you are in the faith; test yourselves. Do you not realize that Christ Jesus is in you--unless, of course, you fail the test? 2 Corinthians 13;5

What kind of test? How can we examine ourselves? Essentially, the Apostle Paul was telling us, no one else can tell you whether you are saved. If you have accepted Christ as your savior, and you fully follow what Jesus taught, "Do not think that I have come to abolish the Law or the Prophets; I have not come to abolish them but to fulfill them." Matthew 5:17

So, Teacher, what are the greatest commandments? "To this Jesus replied: You shall love the Lord your God with all your heart, and with all your soul, and with all your mind. ' This is the greatest and first commandment. Love God above all else. And the second is like it: 'You shall love your neighbor as yourself." Luke 10:27

Dear Savior Jesus, help realize that what I interpret as the world being nasty and horrible to me is my illusionary way of interpreting natural events as being evil forces working against me. So many horrible things that happen start out as insignificant problems that through my failure to Love As you have instructed me to love, are allowed to become my focus. These become my failures in faith, as What we focus on will grow. If we focus on Loving God and our neighbors, the bad events will wither on the vine and the good will triumph in the hearts of all humankind!

Day 41

A Devotional for Understanding and Acceptance

Yesterday, I said we would take a look at number 2 in the list of 6 ways to keep from losing our faith in a world of faithless people. #2 was: Find Inspiration in Biblical Figures. You may have your favorites. I know U have a few. I know there may be some readers that have never really thought about it before. If you have taken inspiration from Biblical figures, please share them with us and tell us why you find them inspirational.

Here are three Biblical figures I have always found to be inspirational. First is Joseph's son of Jacob and Rachel. Upon imprisoning Joseph, the brothers saw a camel caravan carrying spices and perfumes to Egypt and sold Joseph to these merchants.[c] Thereafter the guilty brothers painted goat's blood on Joseph's coat and showed it to Jacob, who therefore believed Joseph had died. (see Genesis 37:12-35). Joseph was ultimately responsible for saving all his family from starvation during a prolonged famine. Even though he was betrayed by his brothers, he never wavered in his faith.

Second is The Apostle Paul, who was a persecutor of early Christians, but had a transformational encounter with Spirit of the Living Christ and became one of the most prolific letter writers of the followers of Jesus. He is revered today as one of the most blessed saints of the early church.

My third inspiring biblical figure is Elizabeth, mother of John the Baptist. In the time of Herod king of Judea there was a priest named Zechariah, who belonged to the priestly division of Abijah; his wife Elizabeth was also a descendant of Aaron. Both of them were righteous in the sight of God, observing all the Lord's commands and decrees blamelessly. But they were childless because Elizabeth was not able to conceive, and they were both very old. (Luke 1:5-7)

But the angel said to him: "Do not be afraid, Zechariah; your prayer has been heard. Your wife Elizabeth will bear you a son, and you are to call him John. He will be a joy and delight to you, and many will rejoice because of his birth, for he will be great in the sight of the Lord. He is never to take wine or other fermented drink, and he will be filled with the Holy Spirit even before he is born. He will bring back many of the people of Israel to the Lord their God. And he will go on before the Lord, in the spirit and power of Elijah, to turn the hearts of the parents to their children and the disobedient to the wisdom of the righteous—to make ready a people prepared for the Lord." Luke 1:11-17)

Heavenly Creator God, thank you for providing so many amazing faithful role models for us to follow. As we examine their lives, we see that the struggle is not new. Through the ages, things have always been difficult for those who love God and desire to be a model Christian and love their neighbor as well. Thank you for forgiving our sins, and please help us forgive others who we may find difficult to forgive. As St. Francis so aptly put it, "for it is in pardoning that we are pardoned." AMEN

Day 42

A Devotional for Understanding and Acceptance

This is the third suggestions of 6 in the list of 6 ways to keep from losing our faith in a world of faithless people. Take Solace in Prayer.

Perhaps the best way to help is to look at prayers directly quoted in the Bible and prayers that have made a difference in our lives. If you have a favorite prayer you would like to share, please feel free to do so.

Here are my favorite prayers.

"Jabez called upon the God of Israel, saying, **'Oh that you would bless me and enlarge my border, and that your hand might be with me, and that you would keep me from harm so that it might not bring me pain!** ' And God granted what he asked" (1 Chronicles 4:10).

Who was Jabez? According to Allaboutprayer.com; The name Jabez means "he causes pain," so we can assume that something about his birth was exceptionally more painful than the usual birth - either physically or emotionally. In Bible times, a name was very important. A name often defined a person's future - what they would become. So perhaps Jabez's mother was predicting her baby's future.

Jesus, of course provided us with what is commonly referred to as the Lord's Prayer:

"This, then, is how you should pray:

"Our Father in heaven, hallowed be your name, your kingdom come, your will be done, on earth as it is in heaven. Give us today our daily bread. And forgive us our debts, as we also have forgiven our debtors. And lead us not into temptation but deliver us from the evil one.

But Jesus was in prayer so often, the prayers recorded are numerous. Here are a few:

Now is my soul troubled; and what shall I say? Father, save me from this hour: but for this cause came I unto this hour. 28 Father, glorify thy name. Then came there a voice from heaven, saying, I have both glorified it, and will glorify it again.

At that time Jesus said, "I praise you, Father, Lord of heaven and earth, because you have hidden these things from the wise and learned and revealed them to little children. Yes, Father, for this is what you were pleased to do. "All things have been committed to me by my Father. Matthew 11:25-27

John: Chapter 17 is a prayer! In chapter 16, Jesus tells his disciples what to expect will happen in the fairly near future. After Jesus said this, he looked toward heaven and prayed: "Father, the hour has come. Glorify Your Son, that Your Son also may glorify You, as You have given Him authority over all flesh, that He should give eternal life to as many as You have given Him. And this is eternal life, that they may know You, the only true God, and Jesus Christ whom You have sent. I have glorified You on the earth. I have finished the work which You have given Me to do. And now, O Father, glorify Me together with Yourself, with the glory which I had with You before the world was.

"I have manifested Your name to the men whom You have given Me out of the world. They were Yours, You gave them to Me, and they have kept Your word. Now they have known that all things which You have given Me are from You. For I have given to them the words which You have given Me; and they have received them, and have known surely that I came forth from You; and they have believed that You sent Me.

"I pray for them. I do not pray for the world but for those whom You have given Me, for they are Yours. And all Mine are Yours, and Yours are Mine, and I am glorified in them. Now I am no longer in the world, but these are in the world, and I come to You. Can we get a HUGE AMEN?

Day 43

A Devotional for Understanding and Acceptance

The fourth of our 6 suggestions is Connect with a Faith-Based Community. I believe we have created a new Faith-Based Community. We have over 100 people who have liked and/or commented on one or more of these Devotional posts. If you are ok with my sharing you name on a future post, please let us all know with a yes: share my name and offer an Amen to the following prayer:

Gracious Savior, thank you for bringing this group of Faithful Followers to this place, at this time, and with such passion for the Amazing-Omnipotent Creators work. We know we could make other choices in our lives but, we choose anew every day to be reverent to Our Awesome Creator God, Savior sent to us, and the Devine Spirit that holds us all in their arms. Protect all who seek your solace, peace and Joy. It is yours alone to even allow this group of Faithful Believers to exist and enjoy the promised eternal life. We need not be concerned for your Acceptance is assured to us by Savior, as he told us all: "There is more than enough room in my Father's home. If this were not so, would I have told you that I am going to prepare a place for you?" John 14:2 Amen

Day 44

A Devotional for Understanding and Acceptance

This is when the going gets tough! How tough are you? Will wilt in the face of suggestions 5 and 6? #5 is simple. Do Good in the World. Why is this so simple? The challenge is not to do good in the world but to make up for doing bad things. It's very simple; **Only Do Good Things!**

Jesus didn't pull any punches. He hits us square, right between our eyes.

"Teacher, which is the greatest commandment in the Law?"

Jesus replied: "'Love the Lord your God with all your heart and with all your soul and with all your mind.' This is the first and greatest commandment. And the second is like it: 'Love your neighbor as yourself.' All the Law and the Prophets hang on these two commandments." Matthew 22:36-40

We must ask ourselves, in each thing I say, do, write, broadcast, or even think, I am commanded to answer this question before I execute the actions: How does what I am going to do, display **the love of God for** all humans, especially those who witness my life, and will they see **how much love and respect I**

<u>have for God,</u> through what I am about to do? This is why this gets so hard. We can no longer behave as if God has made us the decider of guilt or innocence; this would be way too presumptuous and disrespectful of God's sovereignty. We also fail miserably in loving one another as Christ has loved us. If we treat a single person with contempt and disgust, we should forgiveness and remember, we will only receive the level and amount of forgiveness we offer to those we hold in contempt and disgust.

Here is a simple act of kindness that has been prove to heal hurting hearts. Start of with one person for which you have contempt and disgust. Write the name of that person on the top line of a 3 x 5 note card. On the first line under the person's name write down the worst thing about the person. On the next line next worst and continue until you have at least 5 of this person's worst qualities. Now, ask yourself: have I ever been like any of these? Be careful, sometimes our own biggest fault is not recognizing the bad things we've done. Now: pray that your God and Savior might send their divine spirit to cover you with their love and help erase the bad feeling you have and that the spirit will continue to provide you with the strength to resist looking for the bad in that person ever again. Be as sincere as you possibly can. Pray this prayer everyday for 2 weeks and now see how you fell. How does your sincerity level change during those 2 weeks?

Experience tells us that when you do this, you will feel much better than you think you might. When you move on from this experience, I recommend you use 2 note cards for 2 more people. And then 2 more. Follow the same process as above.

Our prayer for today: "Gracious God, help me over come my inability to love and forgive. I often don't realize how closely tied they are. I want to experience your perfect love, offered to me without conditions attached. If I can love others as you have loved me, I know we can change the world." AMEN

Day 45

A Devotional for Understanding and Acceptance

This may be even more difficult than #5 for many people. Suggestion #6 is to Show Compassion. What does the word compassion mean? There are 5 possible responses to the suffering of others. The most crass response is: what is wrong with you- get over it. (Level 1) The next level (level2) is sympathy, which means to truly feel sorry for the person who has been hurt. The third level of response is empathy. An empathic response involves truly feeling the same emotional distress the sufferer is feeling. To have compassion (level 4) means that you not only understand the feelings of another but are ready willing and able to do something about their feelings. There are 2 ways we can show our compassion by fixing what appears to be the cause of the problem (level 4) or actually fixing the problem (level 5). We need both of these for a person to feel better and to remove those obstacles that created the problem. To get to the 6th level requires, in addition to 4 and 5, that we help the person become a new person all together! This is the compassion Christ has asked us all to show.

This is such a huge expectation for us mere humans. That's why we must follow the example of the disciples, especially as they're transitioned from discipleship to being an apostle!

And Jesus went throughout all the cities and villages, teaching in their synagogues and proclaiming the gospel of the kingdom and healing every disease and every affliction. When he saw the crowds, he had compassion for them, because they were harassed and helpless, like sheep without a shepherd. Then he said to his disciples, "The harvest is plentiful, but the laborers are few; therefore, pray earnestly to the Lord of the harvest to send out laborers into his harvest." Matthew 9:35-38

The Book of Acts chronicles the development of early Christian Life. The Apostles became truly Compassionate Followers of Jesus as the Messiah as prophesied in the Old Testament. Acts 4:32-35 tells us about the unity that existed among the Apostles.

All the believers were one in heart and mind. No one claimed that any of their possessions was their own, but they shared everything they had. With great power the apostles continued to testify to the resurrection of the Lord Jesus. And God's grace was so powerfully at work in them all that there were no needy persons among them. For from time to time those who owned land or houses sold them, brought the money from the sales and put it at the apostles' feet, and it was distributed to anyone who had need. And Paul tells us: Be kind and compassionate to one another, forgiving each other, just as in Christ God forgave you. Ephesians 4:32 The Great Commission that Christ charged all of his followers with is:

Then the eleven disciples went to Galilee, to the mountain where Jesus had told them to go. When they saw him, they worshiped him; but some doubted. Then Jesus came to them and said, "All authority in heaven and on earth has been given to me. Therefore go and make disciples of all nations, baptizing them in the name of the Father and of the Son and of the Holy Spirit, and teaching them to obey everything I have commanded you. And surely I am with you always, to the very end of the age." Matthew 28:16-20

We see in the Gospels, Book of Acts of the Apostles, the letters written to the Churches across the region by both Peter and Paul, that compassion was not optional, it was essential. And in the passage above, we see that Jesus instructed the disciples to go out and change lives. Make disciples of all who will listen.

Hear my prayer amazing redeemer, help me achieve the ultimate in meeting my personal responsibility, "fulfilling the Great Commission." The love you have shown us is so powerful, far more powerful than any weapon, let us all LOVE to transform people and in so doing, help us change our world. Let us bring peace on earth, every day in every way to every nation and every home! There is only one race and it is the Human Race! Forgive us, correct us, inspire us so that we will remember how marvelous it feels to be put on the right path, forgiven, redeemed, and changed forevermore! AMEN

Day 46

A Devotional for Understanding and Acceptance

I want to thank everyone who has read any of the first 45 Devotional Posts I've made. I hope that I have challenged your prior mindset regarding salvation and who has the right to pass any judgment on anyone for any behavior, attitude, or political, social, economic, or lifestyle belief that anyone has. As we judge, so shall we be judged. I have grown immensely through this process and I believe I have grown closer and closer to God the Creator, God our Savior, and God the Spirit that asks to reside within our hearts.

Recently I've thought about all the positives I receive from writing and posting these Devotionals. They are numerous. One of the most important outcomes is that I have had to go deep inside my heart and soul and mind to examine what truly is there. I sense a greater closeness to God the Creator and know my salvation is assured. I no longer am concerned as to whether the salvation of any other human being is assured for that is theirs alone to navigate. I can only open my heart, soul, and mind and share what my experiences are. It's each person's responsibility to see for themselves what awaits them in the future.

I choose to not judge others. That is the responsibility of the Creator alone. My wish for the world is that peace will be created by a massive change in heart. I pray that the Heart of Salvation, our Lord Jesus, will truly go **VIRAL** and be the Heart, Soul, and mind and Life Changing Message for all.

Gracious God, I pray that you will touch the heart of every human being on this planet. Yes, everyone needs you: Putin, Trump, Biden, Ayatollah Ali Khamenei, and everyone else! We all fall short. Some want everyone to agree with them and bow down to them, help them see the error in their beliefs! There is only one connector to all that we are meant to be! That is the great Source of Everything that exists. What is power, power is what energy yields. All power and energy is yours alone. We receive it by your grace, and each of us is responsible for using our power for Good! Thank you for putting these ideas out there within our reach. We were told by Jesus that all we have to do is ask, and we will receive, knock and the door will be opened, to seek and we will find! The promise is real. He showed us the way. His way; the way of Truth, Light, Love, and Humility. No one can truly know without allowing Love for All Mankind into their heart. Warm our hearts Dear God and lead us towards an encounter with your Devine Spirit today! We have guarantees as to when our time has come, so touch our hearts today, while we rejoice in your undying HOLY LOVE! AMEN

Day 47

A Devotional for Understanding and Acceptance

When will Christ return and establish the Worldwide, Universe-Wide KINGDOM of Eternal Life! No more suffering! No more pain! Joy and Praise for every human under the watchful eyes of a Loving God. So many people have predicted the date and time so many times. But we should all know better.

Once, having been asked by the Pharisees when the kingdom of God would come, Jesus replied, *"The kingdom of God does not come with your careful observation, nor will people say, 'Here it is,' or 'There it is,' because the kingdom of God is within you." Luke 17:20-21*

Paul says when Christ died on the cross as an atonement for our sins, he (God)" . . . rescued us from the dominion of darkness and brought us into the kingdom of the Son he loves (Colossians 1:13-14) It is in Christ that we become "fellow workers for the kingdom of God." (Colossians 4:11)!

Jesus said, "My kingdom is not of this world. If it were, my servants would fight to prevent my arrest by the Jewish leaders. But now my kingdom is from another place." "You are a king, then!" said Pilate.

Jesus answered, "You say that I am a king. In fact, the reason I was born and came into the world is to testify to the truth. Everyone on the side of truth listens to me." John 18:36-37

And finally, Jesus is quoted in Matthew 24: 36-44. "But about that day or hour no one knows, not even the angels in heaven, nor the Son, but only the Father. As it was in the days of Noah, so it will be at the coming of the Son of Man. For in the days before the flood, people were eating and drinking, marrying, and giving in marriage, up to the day Noah entered the ark; and they knew nothing about what would happen until the flood came and took them all away. That is how it will be at the coming of the Son of Man. Two men will be in the field; one will be taken and the other left. Two women will be grinding with a hand mill; one will be taken and the other left.

"Therefore, keep watch, because you do not know on what day your Lord will come. But understand this: If the owner of the house had known at what time of night the thief was coming, he would have kept watch and would not have let his house be broken into. So, you also must be ready, because the Son of Man will come at an hour when you do not expect him."

Holy Gracious God, let us all give up this strange quest we often have. This quest to decipher exactly when your kingdom will be established on this Earth. That is such folly, when we could use our time so much better, getting to know you and the kingdom of heaven which you placed inside each of us. For as we search for clues in the stars and world events, we miss Your Heavenly presence among us and within us. We can experience your love, which is truly heaven, yet we are so busy trying to think our way into your heavenly presence. When I can love others, unconditionally as you have loved me, even though I know in my heart and soul how undeserving I am, that is when I will have reached the gates of heaven. Thank you, dear Creator God, my gratitude for your sacrifice, is my pathway to salvation. For it is in realizing, that while I have sinned and you are more pure than is possible for a mere human, I am able to surrender my heart, mind, and body to your re-creating of my life, love, and purpose. Help me to set aside my analytical brain so that I might be able to feel your presence in my life! AMEN

Day 48

A Devotional for Understanding and Acceptance

Why have so many young adults left organized religion?

The answer today, is significantly different than it was 40 years ago, although most leaders of formal, organized religious organizations will tell you the problem stems from a lack of faith in a creator. 50 years ago, shortly after I graduated from college, that was probably true. Many of my contemporaries could not see why, anyone would believe that there even was a God. Today, the lack of faith is not in a creator God, but in the institutions that profess to believe in God and the Salvation brought to us all by Jesus. At the same time, those institutions want to paint those entities; God, Savior, and the Spirit that is within us all, into a box that is immutable and out of touch with the message Jesus taught and are clearly documented in the Gospels. But these difficulties, have not significantly changed through the eons and centuries. We continuously face obstacles created by leaders who are more focused on controlling people than leading people to a relationship with God.

In Matthew, we read what Jesus taught on a mountain. We call this 'the Sermon on the Mount.' Jesus taught people that the law was about more than our behavior. For example, one command is: 'Do not murder'. Jesus taught that anger against other people would break this law. The command against adultery included having wrong thinking, sexual thoughts when we look at another person or in other words objectifying men or women. "You have heard that it was said, 'You shall not commit adultery. But I tell you that anyone who looks at a woman lustfully has already committed adultery with her in his heart." Matthew 5:27,28). These commandments are like flashing warning lights . These commands show us how to live. God is perfect, and he wants us to be perfect too, but being only human, we all fall way short. In the Sermon on the Mount, Jesus showed that the *Pharisees had wrong ideas about the law. These people honor me with their lips, but their hearts are far from me. They worship me in vain; their teachings are merely human rules.'" Jesus called the crowd to him and said, "Listen and understand. (Matthew 15:8-10)

Heavenly Creator God: help us all understand that keeping the letter of the law without looking at why the law was created, allows very narrow minded people to ignore the ,spirit of protection, the true loving emotional basis behind the law. Adultery, even the thought of an adulterous act, is an act of thinking of another person as an object to be used. Wishing someone would disappear or die, as a result of an angry response to who they are, what they are, or something they've done or something they represent, disrespects

God's greatest creation, a human being! Please dear God, forgive our failure to learn the very lessons which the Pharisees failed to learn, which resulted in the need for Jesus to come, be crucified, and die for "OUR" SINS! Thank you, Great Redeemer God, for not condemning us to eternal darkness. You are Perfect and we are not. Help us learn, understand, and know how to apply the spirit of your laws, as we begin to realize why those laws were needed. They were needed because we thought we should take priority over others. Once again, Jesus teaches: If you put yourself above others, you will be placed behind those at that time when it really counts. Lead us towards a greater, more positive expression of the perfect, unconditional love you have, do, and continue to show us! AMEN

Day 49

A Devotional for Understanding and Acceptance

Am I a heretic? Are you? Is anyone not a heretic?

A HERETIC is a person who differs in opinion from established religious dogma. According to this definition I found in the Merriam-Webster Dictionary, Jesus was a Heretic! So, we're all the Apostles. And then, the accepted religious beliefs changed and became Roman Catholicism in Europe and many parts of the Middle East (if you ignore Coptic, Greek, and other orthodox churches). Heresy needed to be redefined.

Sometimes, we might need a heretic or 2 or more! John the Baptist, Jesus of Nazareth, Peter, Paul, James, and the others who followed Jesus, according to the Jewish Pharisees, were Heretics. There were, undoubtedly, many heretics that challenged the accepted religious order at many different points in time from the third Century (CE) until 1517 when Martin Luther nailed his 95 theses (Disputation on the Power and Efficacy of Indulgences) on the Door of the All-Saints Cathedral in Wittenberg, Germany. This resulted in Luther being charged with heresy, a trial, conviction, And Luther's Excommunication from the Roman Catholic Church. Of Course, the real heretical concept here was Indulgences. Jesus wanted us all to understand that you could not buy your way into heaven, nor could you buy a relative's way into heaven. Thus, the Reformation began, and Protest(ant) Churches began popping up across Germany and other reformers began an ongoing challenge to the way Rome was interpreting what Christians must do to be saved and enter heaven.

Since 1517 and the beginning of the reformation movement, we have continuously seen people challenging the way organized religion has demanded how we conduct our lives. Methodism, Calvinism, Evangelism, Anabaptism, Pentecostalism, and Mormonism. These are just a few of the "heretical" deviations that have taken their own special style of Christianity and created new ways to worship God. As each of these create their own way to determine how we should behave based on their own special Bible interpretations, we will see those who disagree, so we will continue to have organized religious leaders label those who disagree as Heretics!

So, I proudly accept the mantle of heretic! In the Great Tradition of Jesus, the Apostle Paul, St. Peter (Simon) Martin Luther, John Wesley, John Calvin, and so many others who only wanted a more pure connection with the heart of Jesus, let's all question religious authority of any human.

Precious Jesus, hear our prayer! When all else fails, we understand that it may be necessary to go against the grain. When those in control of our institutions abuse the power, they've been allowed to have, we have the responsibility to call them on it.

Whether those leaders of governmental, religious, cultural, service, educational, industrial, or any other human endeavor, start to leave out some critical information, in order to fool some of the people, feed the biases of others, and/or pit philosophical points of against one another, we know it's time to introduce some alternative thinking. We know that religious leaders during the few years of your ministry called you a blasphemer, a Heretic, and more. (Read Matthew 26:59-65) Let us each take up our cross and follow your example. (Read Matthew 16:24-26) Lord help us remember that we cannot experience safety, security, or liberty if we allow leaders to use the letter of the very laws created by God to punish people when the punishment issued runs counter to the 2 Greatest Commandments we've been given. We all too often forget that the concept of cruel and unusual punishment was openly defied by You, dear savior, when you challenged the accusers Toby saying, let the one among you without sun cast the first stone. You so clearly saw the ruse that leaders of your day employed and their complete misuse of the very reason those laws were made. Every once in a while, a little heresy is needed. If we get the idea wrong, we promise to admit our error and seek forgiveness! Let us study the examples that are provided in so many places in the Bible. AMEN

Day 50

A Devotional for Understanding and Acceptance

If I'm a Heretic, does that mean I can do anything I want?

Yesterday I talked about the Heretics of the past! You'll notice in that devotional offering, all of the heretics mentioned were trying to bring a closer relationship to God for the people in their lives. Now you may disagree with some or even all of this, but do not mistake your opinion with meaning that anyone one of these people having bad intentions. That would be excessively judgmental on our part.

If the decisions you make harm others physically, emotionally, intellectually, psychologically, or spiritually, you are not being heretical, you are being a bully. If what your intentions are can be construed as good, but cause physical, emotional, or psychological pain and damage, you are not a heretic, you are a Bully building a cult of followers who just might create chaos and more pain and suffering.

I realize that there may be a very thin line that separates heretics trying to improve our relay with God and those individuals trying to get people to worship them rather than God. Those false prophets will tell you what ever will put them in a good light with people but do not speak with authority from God. There have always been false prophets but their deceitful ways are always followed by very definite proof of the lies they tell. Unfortunately, some people refuse to face the truth and will follow them into self-destruction. Not all heretics, in fact most do not have anything but their own interest in mind.

How can we tell the difference between someone who is heretic in the eyes of a church but is truly a messenger inspired by the word of God, and real heretic that who might even be supported in their ideas by a church but who never has really listened carefully to God's word? "Then many false prophets will rise up and deceive many" (Matthew 24:11). There's a simple test. Just ask those people why we should believe what is being said. In Matthew 10:16 and Luke 10:3, Jesus warned His followers about "wolves" who would be openly hostile to the Gospel. But Matthew 7 presents a more subtle threat—wolves disguised as sheep. "Beware of false prophets, who come to you in sheep's clothing, but inwardly they are ravenous wolves" The real messenger of God will always tell you, don't believe this because I say it, read what Jesus had to say about what I've said, and then pray that Spirit of the Living God will guide your thoughts and bring to an understanding of what real, true, and aligned with what Jesus asked of us. The prayer I'm talking about is what you do, in a quiet place and you don't even have let anyone else know what you are praying about.

Here's my most common prayer for guidance about what I should believe. "Heavenly Creator God, I pray that my thoughts and meditations will open my mind, heart, and soul to your thoughts, instruction, and desires. Please let your spirit wash upon and over me so that I might feel what is right and gain true knowing, understanding and develop the ability to do what you desire for my life. Give me the strength of mind, body, spirit, and faith to keep moving in the right direction and always forward in Love of You and my fellow humans and in direction of a more perfect faith in You and Your promises to all people, from all nations, all races, and all languages. AMEN

Day 51

A Devotional for Understanding and Acceptance

What should I Accept? And What Do I Need to Understand?

First, I truly Hope that everyone understands that we all have so much more in common than we do that is different. Our experiences are so similar that if we really look closely, we just might be shocked at how similar those experiences are. It doesn't matter where we are from, what we eat, what color our skin is, what type of building we call home, what language we speak, or how we worship or do not worship God! It's how we each react to those experiences that can either demonstrate our deep love for our Creator, or our disdain for that Creator!

Whatever ever we do out of Love for God, must be in alignment with true acts of Love. If I truly Love A Person, I will never intentionally "HURT" that person. Whether I hurt a person or not, is not my call! That will be determined by THAT OTHER HUMAN BEING! If I find out that my actions have hurt someone, I can only demonstrate my Christ-Centered Unconditional Love by seeking forgiveness. Part of my true acceptance of the forgiveness offered to me requires me to seek ways to change my responses to that experience. This is my ultimate Responsibility.

Think of Responsibility as my Ability to Respond to what I experience in any way I see fit. I have that Ability! I am not a robot. How does Christ want us to Respond to any situation? With Loving Kindness and redirection. When Christ kept the mob from stoning an adulterous Woman, was he giving the Green-light to adultery. Let's revisit that scene:

The teachers of the law and the Pharisees brought in a woman caught in adultery. They made her stand before the group and said to Jesus, "Teacher, this woman was caught in the act of adultery. In the Law Moses commanded us to stone such women. Now what do you say?" They were using this question as a trap, in order to have a basis for accusing him.

But Jesus bent down and started to write on the ground with his finger. When they kept on questioning him, he straightened up and said to them, "Let any one of you who is without sin be the first to throw a stone at her." Again he stooped down and wrote on the ground. At this, those who heard began to go away one at a time, the older ones first, until only Jesus was left, with the woman still standing there. Jesus straightened up and asked her, "Woman, where are they? Has no one condemned you?"

No one, sir," she said.

*"Then neither do I condemn you," Jesus declared. "Go now and **leave your life of sin.**" John 8: 3-11*

Jesus forgives us, no matter how heinous the transgressions. What he wants to see, is that we change. He wants us to Leave our life of sin behind and behave in a Response Able (responsible) WAY! What are the 2 Greatest Commandments: Love God with all your Heart, Mind, Spirit, Strength! And just a Jesus did, Love Our Neighbors: not just the people who are exactly like us, but he opened up our neighborhoods to be all inclusive!

How we respond to similar situations differently can easily demonstrated by the Governors of the 2 states where Barb and I spent most of our time. Michigan and Florida. Now the very Liberal people think the Governor of Michigan is Mother Theresa and the Governor of Florida is Satan himself! Of course, the very conservative people think the opposite is true. In reality, they are both approaching the same situations with a very similar desired outcome. However, how you achieve that outcome is incredibly different. Our reality is what we see as our best response to our experiences. The truth of a conservative is different from the truth of a liberal. "Nobody's right if everybody's wrong!" How would Jesus respond to this dichotomy? He might just say: "Nobody's right if everybody's wrong!" (Stephen Still-For What it's Worth) Or he might suggest we all sing the Hymn "All Hail the Power of Jesus' Name":

All hail the power of Jesus' name! Let every **tongue** and every **tribe** be responsive to his call, to him all majesty ascribe, and crown him, crown him, crown him, crown him Lord of all!

Hear our prayer oh Great and Glorious God and our Savior Jesus Christ, help us be accepting of the amazing diversity You created in our world. Help us also to seek understanding rather than expect everyone else will understand us. Help us realize that the amazingness that is your creation, exists not for us to plunder and abuse but that it is a sacred trust given to us to sustain all of mankind. Help us finally realize that our purpose is to sustain the joy brought into the world upon your entrance in Bethlehem. Let us shed tears of exultant happiness often and with gratitude for what you did for mankind. Please let the opposites sides truly forgive one another, for as I look at the politics in America, I see both sides making the same argument from two different directions. Nobody's Right if Everybody's Wrong! AMEN

Day 52

A Devotional for Understanding and Acceptance

Is God's Day the same length as an Earth day? You decide!

That question was posed to me, in the fall of 1972, that just a little over 50 years ago. One the students in a section of 7th grade science was trying to balance what we were talking about in class with what his youth pastor was saying in Church. We were talking about light years, the distance light travels in 1 year is considered a light year. Since the speed of light is 186,282 miles per second, or 670,615,200 miles per hour! In a day, light travels 16,094,600,000 miles. In a year, light travels 5,874,529,000,000 miles. So, when on the first day, God created Light; perhaps the Emission of light, all at once would correspond if a huge bursting forth of all the energy of the universe in one massive letting loose of energy. (A Big Bang) That would some big bursting forth of energy. On the second day the sky was created, (it would seem to be a little out of order, but that is not something to quibble about now), and the third day the seas were separated from the dry land (which again seems just a bit out of a logical sequence)and the 4th day all that light was put in place in the sun and all of the glowing objects in the sky, such as stars and the moon. And then, living things were created on the 5th and 6th days, with humanity coming into being in the last act of creation.

So, this student was confused, if the closest stars to Earth are more than 4.5 quadrillions miles away, and it the furthest stars are maybe a billions times further away than that, after 6 of Earth's days, as we know them today, the earliest people would have to wait at least 4.5 years before they would have been able to see the closest star, besides our own Sun!

My response to the inquiry 50+ years ago was, God has never, in all that has been written, insisted that divinity is based on logic and the reporting based on revelations shared with those who wrote of how things happened, has been the best interpretation of what was revealed by humans whose capacity for explaining it all was limited by a lack of understanding of scientific discoveries of the time, and certainly lack knowledge of all that has been discovered and postulated over the last 150 years. So trying to compare Biblical Creation timelines to a logical sequence of events and the timelines that science suggests, is like trying to store light in a glass jar! Light is energy and a glass jar can only contain things that possess energy; matter. Trying to logically sequence things was not what the writers of the creation story we're trying to do. They were making their best attempt, to explain an amazing, extraordinary event based on what was revealed to them at the time.

they were trying. We cannot try to logically determine whether or not the Creation Story is a True Story or just a story.

Faith is about believing even if the facts and logic point in another direction. Faith cannot be swayed by logic. It often defies logic. Data and statistics don't require faith, other than faith in the accuracy and integrity of the person or people measuring what we think is important. There's an old saying that says figures don't lie. But you know that sometimes liars are in charge of doing the calculating. Not everything that is measured is important, and not everything that is important is measured.

Humble yourselves, therefore, under God's mighty hand, that he may lift you up in due time. Cast all your anxiety on him because he cares for you. — 1 Peter 5:6-7

Hear Our Prayer oh Gracious Creator God, help us discern the truth about your amazing Creative power and might. Logical cannot explain how you created or how much time it might have taken to create all that exists. We know you are a living God and the Act of Creation continues today. For YOU, time does not exist. For YOU a minute can last centuries. For YOU a billion years is the same as a minute, a day, or a month. Help us not get all tied in nots over Logic for the life, all by itself is not logical! No matter how we slice the PIE OF LIFE as we know it, the only logical answer is to have faith in a POWER AND CREATIVE FORCE, THAT IN THE

FACE OF AWFUL ANTI-PROGRESSIVE, OFTEN NEGATIVE DATA, continues to drive life ever onward towards better, more abundant, and more fulfilling lives! We praise and glorify YOU against all logic and data and statistics! Love is not logical but you created us so that love is far healthiest than mistrust, hated, violence and ridicule. We faithfully sing: PRAISE GOD FROM WHOM ALL BLESSINGS FLOW. PRAISE GOD ALL CREATURES HERE BELOW. PRAISE GOD, ABOVE YOU HEAVENLY HOSTS! PRAISE GOD THE CREATOR, PRAISE GOD THE CREATOR-SAVIOR SON, and PRAISE GOD THE CREATOR SPIRIT! AMEN

Day 53

A Devotional for Understanding and Acceptance

How many angels can dance on the head of a pin?

During the reformation, it was argued that Catholic (Papists as the we're right and your wrong reformist like to call them) theological scholars wasted their time on these unimportant ideas rather than solve the problems of the suffering throngs of people throughout the world. In mocking the Catholic scholars, the radical reformers forgot and important aspect of the reform movement. Jesus himself might be called a reformer, but he never lost sight of the Goal! Jesus was in pursuit of the salvation of all and would not mock them. Jesus believed in redirecting their focus! How many times did Jesus use the questions that his critics asked to make his point about how we should Love God and Love one another.

So many people have tried to trick others into answering questions in a way that will reveal the true nature of individual ignorance or lack of authority. Every time the Religious Leaders tried to trip up Jesus, they failed. Here's an example from Luke 20: 27-40.

"Some of the Sadducees, who say there is no resurrection, came to Jesus with a question. 'Teacher,' they said, 'Moses wrote for us that if a man's brother dies and leaves a wife but no children, the man must marry the widow and raise up offspring for his brother. Now there were seven brothers. The first one married a woman and died childless. The second and then the third married her, and in the same way the seven died, leaving no children. Finally, the woman died too. Now then, at the resurrection whose wife will she be, since the seven were married to her?'

Jesus replied, 'The people of this age marry and are given in marriage. But those who are considered worthy of taking part in the age to come and in the resurrection from the dead will neither marry nor be given in marriage, and they can no longer die; for they are like the angels. They are God's children, since they are children of the resurrection. But in the account of the burning bush, even Moses showed that the dead rise, for he calls the Lord 'the God of Abraham, and the God of Isaac, and the God of Jacob.' He is not the God of the dead, but of the living, for to him all are alive."

My Prayer is for every person to realize that our purpose in life is to Love and serve God. If someone fails in that purpose, it is not our responsibility to punish them. I have served on Juries before. I realize when I am asked to do so, I am not doing God's work, I am doing the work of this world. Help us to not confuse our civic duty with what God asks of me. Dear Savior Lord Jesus, your expectations of me are a difficult path to follow, you never shied away from telling us that. Because we are imperfect, I ask that you forgive our failures and become our savior and redeem us from our own failures. Although we do understand our failure, we too often forget that we have yet to have the divine status of an angel bestowed upon us. Someday, we will rejoice in the company of our Loved Ones and the heavenly hosts shall reveal the evermore to us, one and all. AMEN

Day 54

A Devotional for Understanding and Acceptance

Over the Centuries, there have been many situations where Christianity has been spread through the use of violent means. Personally, I believe this was wrong. I don't believe this is what God wants and I don't believe there is a Biblical basis for these actions. If there was, please explain to me, with citations from any one of them, or our Lord Jesus himself, why not one of the of the Apostles directed their followers to band together and take on the Roman Empire. Certainly, if the goal was to spread the Gospels by any method possible, Jesus would have instructed us to do so!

The most commonly quoted verse justifying using violence to spread the Gospels is Matthew, 11:12 "And from the days of John the Baptist until the present time, the kingdom of heaven has endured violent assault, and violent men seize it by force." However, in Luke 17:20-21 it says "Once, on being asked by the Pharisees when the kingdom of God would come, Jesus replied, "The coming of the kingdom of God is not something that can be observed, You won't be able to say, 'Here it is!' or 'It's over there!' For the Kingdom of God is already among you." Many Scholars believe that Jesus was referring to himself, he was there among them to provide the pathway to God's Kingdom, and as that pathway, we know the violence he suffered. The kingdom of heaven was, indeed, taken by violent men.

If Jesus had wanted the Kingdom of God spread by violent means, he would have allowed his followers the protect him. But in Luke 22: 49-51 we read: "When Jesus' followers saw what was going to happen, they said, 'Lord, should we strike with our swords?' And one of them struck the servant of the high priest, cutting off his right ear.

But Jesus answered, 'No more of this!' And he touched the man's ear and healed him." Jesus was not a violent man, in fact the most violent action he displayed was overturning the tables of the money changers at the temple. Matthew 21:12-13 Jesus entered the temple courts and drove out all who were buying and selling there. He overturned the tables of the money changers and the benches of those selling doves. "It is written," he said to them, "'My house will be called a house of prayer,' but you are making it 'a den of robbers."

Gracious God, Creator and Parent of all humanity, We do ask that your will be done! There are many of us who believe that the violence perpetrated to convert people to Followers of Christ was an error in judgement by many well-meaning but wrong minded people in the past. Help us all realize that conversion is not a physical act but a spiritual act. You can make me say I believe but if my spirit is not committed to the salvation offered, my allegiance can be easily swayed. Teach me to love others as you have Loved me and in peace, love, and unity, I know we can change the world! AMEN

Day 55

A Devotional for Understanding and Acceptance

How are our habits created? And how can we change them to reduce disease and pain?

It's easy to understand that a drug, such as an opiate, if taken for enough days in a row, will create a chemical dependence on the drug. For your body to function you must have the drug. You now have a drug habit. It's a little more difficult to see how something that does not create a direct alteration in your body chemistry, can cause a long term habit. If your body does not require the drug to continue to function, why do people keep up that same habit. Over eating, becoming lethargic, reacting to seemingly none threatening events in an angry way, needing to have everything go your way; if you do these things for more than 5 or 6 days, you begin to feel like you will be ok, you just have to give yourself enough time and you'll get over it. If it goes on for several weeks, this behavior becomes a temperament. If this goes on for several months, this behavior becomes a personality trait.

When you've hit this level, a behavior that describes you, becomes a personality trait. Now, it is this personality trait that is causing you to behave the way you do. To change this, you must turn the whole situation upside down. You got this way by justifying what you do based on the circumstances that you reacted to that led to this behavior trait. When you still had a clear and simple choice as to how you would react to conditions in your environment, you originally, without clearly thinking it through, concerning which response will be most productive and which responses will cause you the most difficulty, you picked a response that was influenced by your emotional state at that time. How you responded ignored what would be most helpful and quite often people select a response based on what ever emotion popped up at the time. We are quite able to pick a response that is most aligned with our future goals and how your reaction will either help or hurt your chances. However, too many people choose responses that cause harm to themselves as well as others.

What we now know is that, if a very negative responses to any situation is allowed to be the most common response you have to specific events, that can be very harmful to one's own health. You can make yourself sick with these negative responses. If we can make by ourselves sick with the way we respond to events we are confronted with, then isn't it possible that we can reverse this, and make ourselves heal by changing our response to these very same events and many other events from a negative response to a positive, life affirming response. We find many Biblical statements that tell us what attitude we should have.

Finally, brothers, whatever is true, whatever is honorable, whatever is just, whatever is pure, whatever is lovely, whatever is commendable, if there is any excellence, if there is anything worthy of praise, think about these things. Philippians 4:8

Let all bitterness and wrath and anger and clamor and slander be put away from you, along with all malice. Be kind to one another, tenderhearted, forgiving one another, as God in Christ forgave you. Ephesians 4:31-32

"Therefore do not worry, saying, 'What shall we eat?' or 'What shall we drink?' or 'What shall we wear?' For after all these things the Gentiles seek. For your heavenly Father knows that you need all these things. But seek first the kingdom of God and His righteousness, and all these things shall be added to you. Therefore, do not worry about tomorrow, for tomorrow will worry about its own things. Sufficient for the day is its own trouble. Matthew 6:31-35

Hear my prayer Creator God! Jesus, your Son, was able to heal the sick, lame, and even raise people from death. He was able to restore sight and hearing. He also passed on to his Disciples the same ability. What was critically important was that was that each person healed maintained the attitude described in Philippians, Ephesians, and by Jesus himself as recorded in Matthew. Maintaining a strong positive attitude and truly believing that our faith can heal us must precede healing. Each person healed by Jesus and his disciples had the faith, the attitude, and then turned their life over to the Savior. Help all who read this have that powerful faith and the powerful Love that Jesus and the Amazing Creator God have and continue to show for us. Please help us all have the faith and the strength of attitude that will allow us to unleash the power of our own biology to reverse the negative health trends that make life more challenging than we all believe it should be! AMEN

Day 56

A Devotional for Understanding and Acceptance

Why should I care about people who refuse to change their ways?

There are people who truly take advantage of people who want to help them. There are people who do horrible, unspeakable things to others. There are people who have been given so many chances, it seems like a complete waste of everyone's time and energy to even try to help them. So why should we make the effort to even try?

In my years of teaching and administrating schools, I was often accused of having a father Flanagan complex. Father Flanagan ran a school for orphans and often troubled boys. Father Flanagan said: "There are no bad boys. There is only bad environment, bad training, bad example, bad thinking." There were many teachers who told me I gave kids too many chances. But, my sense of the circumstances that so many kids face is quite simple: "We can help kids understand how to change the world around them in a very positive way, or we can allow them to become a negative influence and cause serious problems for our local people. "The latter of these two will cost us in money, time, and overall community wellbeing. Over my career, I've chosen to help as many kids as I can.

What has happened to these kids! I think I'll let them speak up and tell you what they've done and where they might have ended up had we not cared! And here's the Biblical basis for everything I did over my 40 + years working with kids.

Train up a child in the way he should go; even when he is old, he will not depart from it. Proverbs: 22:6

Behold, children are a heritage from the Lord, the fruit of the womb a reward. Like arrows in the hand of a warrior are the children of one's youth. Blessed is the man who fills his quiver with them! He shall not be put to shame when he speaks with his enemies in the gate. Psalm: 127:3-5

"See that you do not despise one of these little ones. For I tell you that in heaven their angels always see the face of my Father who is in heaven. Matthew 18:10

Heavenly Creator God, let us not forget what Jesus taught about children. If we fail them, we fail Jesus. Help us to do whatever it takes to never let a child fall into the failure cycle. This is not only a waste of a great deal of money, but it is also an Affront to Gods creation! Let us be all that we can be and help every child succeed! AMEN

Day 57

A Devotional for Understanding and Acceptance

When you look into the eyes of another person, what do you see?

For many of us, what we see will depend on our perception of the person whose eyes we look into. If we perceive the person to be our nemesis, we just might see the devil himself. What do you think Jesus saw in the eyes of those he came into contact with? In truth, we know what he saw. In the eyes of the Centurion who had a gravely ill daughter, he saw love and faith. Roman officers were not friends of the average Jewish Carpenter , so most people of Jesus' day would have seen evil in that centurion's eyes. In the eyes of the Samaritan woman at the well, he saw compassion and caring for a foreign traveler on the road. Most Jews thought of Samaritans as traitors and lacking true allegiance to Israel. Even though they were from the original tribes of Israel, they probably were as different as very conservative republicans and very liberal democrats. But Jesus looked past political alliances and looked into the soul of each person to find where the good was!

I challenge each of us, look into the heart of those you profoundly disagree with and find the true potential for goodness there. As a faith, we can never be whole and holy as Jesus desires until we get beyond petty differences and start help us all find the good in one another.

The poor and homeless:

"The Spirit of the Lord is on me, because he has anointed me to proclaim good news to the poor" Luke 4:18

Looking at his disciples, he said: "Blessed are you who are poor, for yours is the kingdom of God" Luke 6:20

But when you give a banquet, invite the poor, the crippled, the lame, the blind, and you will be blessed. Although they cannot repay you, you will be repaid at the resurrection of the righteous" Luke 14:13-14

The Unclean:

A man with leprosy came to him and begged him on his knees, "If you are willing, you can make me clean."

Jesus was indignant. He reached out his hand and touched the man. "I am willing," he said. "Be clean!" Immediately the leprosy left him, and he was cleansed. Jesus sent him away at once with a strong warning: "See that you don't tell this to anyone. But go, show yourself to the priest and offer the sacrifices that Moses commanded for your cleansing, as a testimony to them." Instead, he went out and began to talk freely, spreading the news. As a result,

Jesus could no longer enter a town openly but stayed outside in lonely places. Yet the people still came to him from everywhere.

Holy Creator God, help us each move past our truly petty differences. Help us understand that the only true freedom any of us has is the freedom to choose how we accept or reject our neighbor and with what intensity that acceptance or rejection will take place. Since everyone is our neighbor and we have been commanded to Love Our Neighbor, and Love God, let us love one another as fervently as You, our Creator God, have loved us. Help us to always look for the good in one another. And help us stop telling those who follow your commandments to Love on another, foolish idealists! DREAMERS IF YOU WILL! Help us understand that when Your Son, Jesus told us that the Kingdom of God is here, right now, among us, he meant it. If we only look for your kingdom within each person we encounter; OH, WHAT AN AMAZING WORLD THIS WOULD BE! AMEN

Day 58

A Devotional for Understanding and Acceptance

If I'm sad or depressed, how can I dig myself out of the darkness I am in?

This question has been asked of me by more than one person over the years. There is only one correct answer to this question. Stop digging! Only 2 things can happen if you continue to dig, you can get deeper into the darkness or create an unstable tunnel that is sure to collapse. You got into the hole of despair and depression by digging into some seriously ugly stuff. Throw yourself a lifeline of fresh air and let the lightness of joy float you out.

Your soul is buoyed or weighed down by our thoughts. If you are constantly thinking of the pain and suffering of the past, your soul will be dark and heavy. If you change your focus from pain and suffering towards beauty and joy, you will find an incredible lightness and will feel more joy than sadness, more inner beauty than ugliness, and you will find grace where desolation and hopelessness once dominated.

As Jesus was walking along, He saw a man who had been blind from birth. "Rabbi," His disciples asked Him, "why was this man born blind? Was it because of his own sins or his parents' sins?" "It was not because of his sins or his parents' sins," Jesus answered. "This happened so the power of God could be seen in him. John 9:1-3

Jesus was clearly telling us all, our health is not a result of sin, but always provides an opportunity to demonstrate God's power, and his continuous care. Depression is caused by a chemical imbalance, this is most commonly caused by habitually focusing on the negative emotions of fear, sorrow, despair, and sadness. These emotions trigger the production of cortisol which is biologically designed to help the body prepare for either fighting off a dangerous enemy or running away from them. If we survive this difficulty but continue to focus on that event for a week or more, we put ourselves into a very bad mood which keeps the cortisol flowing and over stimulates our sadness response, or results in temporary depression. If we allow that emotion to linger for a few months, it becomes a temperament and if it goes on for more than a few months, it becomes a personality trait. Can a personality trait be altered? It most certainly can! Saul of Tarsus was an angry, hateful, violently aggressive persecutor of early Christians. His encounter with the Spirit of the living God, and the Glorious Savior, transformed him into a an Apostle for the Loving, Peaceful, Transformative Christ. Not every angry person will have such a quick transformation. In fact, most people have so closed off their minds to spiritual encounters, transformative experiences have become more difficult than ever.

We can learn from Martha and Mary in Luke 10:38-42:

As Jesus and His disciples were on their way, He came to a village where a woman named Martha opened her home to Him. She had a sister called Mary, who sat at the Lord's feet listening to what He said. But Martha was distracted by all the preparations that had to be made. She came to Him and asked, "Lord, do You not care that my sister has left me to do the work by myself? Tell her to help me!"

"Martha, Martha," the Lord answered, "you are worried and upset about many things, but few things are needed— or indeed only one. Mary has chosen what is better, and it will not be taken away from her."

Our focus on what we worry about causes stress, and we should let go of what worries us.

But those who trust in the Lord will find new strength. They will soar high on wings like eagles, they will run and not grow weary. They will walk and not faint. – Isaiah 40:31

If we will simply turn our focus towards our Joy, rather than sadness, we will ignite the joy chemicals within our own bodies. We know these as Oxytocin, Serotonin, and Dopamine. Oxytocin is the love hormone in our body and creates a feeling of well-being and a sense of safety. Serotonin is the calmness hormone and allows us to look at difficult situations and find a way forward. And dopamine allows us to appreciate what we have and brings joy to our existence.

Dear Jesus, help us find Love, Security, and Happiness rather than hatred, instability, and despair. Help us all remember the delight we found as a child, even amongst the most difficult of times. When the world seemed to the adults around us, to be crumbling into ruin, (and remember, every generation forgets how much havoc they created and truly believes the next generation is the worst ever) we still found time to enjoy the moment, for in our eyes there was nothing other than now!

"That is why I tell you not to worry about everyday life— whether you have enough food and drink, or enough clothes to wear. Isn't life more than food, and your body more than clothing? Look at the birds. They don't plant or harvest or store food in barns, for your heavenly Father feeds them. And aren't you far more valuable to him than they are? Can all your worries add a single moment to your life?" Matthew 6:25-27 Help us remember that The Creator loves us, and when all else fails, we can turn towards the Devine presence within us all! God wants to be in a relationship with us and will if we quiet our minds, open our hearts, and let the spirit wash over us. AMEN

Day 59

A Devotional for Understanding and Acceptance

Which do you like to spend your time with most, People, things, or ideas?

I was reviewing the text of a book I've been writing and continue to make improvements on, and one chapter spends s good amount of time talking about our preferences. Take a moment to really think about the question posed at the beginning of this devotional. Some people like people enough but might be a little uncomfortable with their social skills. So, they may prefer to serve people by fixing things, building things, or inventing things. And then there are folks who feel like they are all thumbs and feel like they have to rely on others to get things the way the feel the need them. And then there are people, full of ideas. They're always thinking and trying to figure out how to best explain what they see in the world.

We need all of these people. However, we must remember that the reason for ideas and things are not to please the idea person or the thing maker or fixer. And the reason for people to really care about and for other problem is not about "me!" And I do mean the little me (the EGO). Our little me can be very hurtful because the little often does not consider others while it's orchestrating the world around that little me.

I'm talking about doing things because we like people and the selflessness of the "BIG ME!" The "BIG ME" is that part of us Jesus talked about continuously.

"I can do nothing on my own. As I hear, I judge, and my judgment is just, because I seek not my own will but the will of him who sent me." John 5:31 Jesus was not here to glorify himself, but to do God's Will.

So if there is any encouragement in Christ, any comfort from love, any participation in the Spirit, any affection and sympathy, complete my joy by being of the same mind, having the same love, being in full accord and of one mind. Do nothing from selfish ambition or conceit, but in humility count others more significant than yourselves. Let each of you look not only to his own interests, but also to the interests of others. Have this mind among yourselves, which is yours in Christ Jesus, ...Philippians 2:1-10

Jesus our Savior, we realize that our Heavenly, Holy Lord God, needs each of us to remember our purpose. It is to glorify The Creator and the amazing creation of which we each are a part. Thank you for helping us all, and let us never forget, all are equal in the eyes of God, and the only thing can put us in a lesser position is our own desire to be more important than others. No matter what our calling, there would be no need for anyone's calling if there were not people who desired to have access to that calling. Bless us dear creator God, for you alone truly know our hearts. Give us a clean heart Oh God and renew a right spirit with in us! AMEN

Day 60

A Devotional for Understanding and Acceptance

Who or What is The real me?

This question is a difficult one to answer, if you do not consider yourself to be a spiritual being as the Apostle Paul did. Paul wanted all Christians to consider the true impact of our Savior in our lives when he said, "I have been crucified with Christ. It is no longer I who live, but Christ who lives in me. And the life I now live in the flesh I live by faith in the Son of God, who loved me and gave himself for me." Galatians 2:20 Without the promise of a spiritual life beyond our days here in the flesh, we all would struggle with an incredible Identity Crisis.

Therefore, if anyone is in Christ, they are a new creation. The old has passed away; behold, the new has come. 2 Corinthians 5:17

Or do you not know that your body is a temple of the Holy Spirit within you, whom you have from God? You are not your own! 1 Corinthians 6:19

I am the vine; you are the branches. Those who abide in me and I in them, will bear much fruit, for apart from me you can do nothing. John 15:5

Gracious Creator God: With these words, we clearly hear that we are part of the living essence of Christ, who is one with The Creator God! We do have to even put out any effort, we need only accept the life force of Christ, and truly understand that God Created all, and at the head if Creation us Christ, and the Spiritual Source of life flies from God to each of us through Christ. Whether we choose to accept Christ as the vine through which all needs for life flow or not, it is clear, not one gets to God except through the Vine. Once we realize and accept the Source, our lives will be forever changed. Thank you for allowing us to receive this amazing message! We understand that true Joy and Happiness comes to us through the Vine that is the Christ! AMEN

Day 61

A Devotional for Understanding and Acceptance

When are we truly at our best as human beings?

And the Word became flesh and dwelt among us, and we have seen his glory, glory as of the only Son from the Father, full of grace and truth." John 1:14 As we attempt to Carry out God's will, we often are trying to coerce God's will into our own selfish plans. We need to filter our plans through God's Plan! Remember, God's Plan is so simple, but it can be hard to stick to it. We too often want to say, "I know God would not want me to enable this bad behavior so, I think we ought to punish the people who do these things that we know are WRONG! Of course the greatest sun of all is "thinking we know what God really wants, and certainly God does not really want us to, oh wait!

"Then the King will say to those on his right, 'Come, you who are blessed by my Father, inherit the Kingdom prepared for you from the creation of the world. For I was hungry, and you fed me. I was thirsty, and you gave me a drink. I was a stranger, and you invited me into your home. I was naked, and you gave me clothing. I was sick, and you cared for me. I was in prison, and you visited me.'

"Then these righteous ones will reply, 'Lord, when did we ever see you hungry and feed you? Or thirsty and give you something to drink? Or a stranger and show you hospitality? Or naked and give you clothing? When did we ever see you sick or in prison and visit you?' "And the King will say, 'I tell you the truth, when you did it to one of the least of these my brothers and sisters,[c] you were doing it to me!' "Then the King will turn to those on the left and say, 'Away with you, you cursed ones, into the eternal fire prepared for the devil and his demons. For I was hungry, and you didn't feed me. I was thirsty, and you didn't give me a drink. I was a stranger, and you didn't invite me into your home. I was naked, and you didn't give me clothing. I was sick and in prison, and you didn't visit me.' "Then they will reply, 'Lord, when did we ever see you hungry or thirsty or a stranger or naked or sick or in prison, and not help you?' "And he will answer, 'I tell you the truth, when you refused to help the least of these my brothers and sisters, you were refusing to help me.' Matthew 25:34-45

Jesus our Savior; I pray that we will be reminded daily that the route to salvation uses only love for fuel. The love we show is the love that we will receive! Hatred, meanness, and imposing our own will rather than the Loving Will if God, will put stumbling blocks in our path. For us to achieve salvation, it is imperative that we, GET OUT OF OUR OWN WAY! If I offer forgiveness and Love, I will receive forgiveness and Love. If I leave only hate and condemnation, I will receive only Hate and condemnation. Loving God, forgive my impertinence and help me give freely of the unconditional Love you have so graciously give me. AMEN

Day 62

A Devotional for Understanding and Acceptance

What did Jesus say about Political Leaders?

Throughout the 3 years of Jesus' ministry, Jesus was dealing with a hostile political environment. His homeland was occupied by the Roman Empire's ruling Governor Pilate, and the Pharisees were after Jesus to discredit him.

And they sent to him some of the Pharisees and some of the Herodians, to trap him in his talk. And they came and said to him, "Teacher, we know that you are true and do not care about anyone's opinion. For you are not swayed by appearances, but truly teach the way of God. Is it lawful to pay taxes to Caesar, or not? Should we pay them, or should we not?" But, knowing their hypocrisy, he said to them, "Why put me to the test? Bring me a denarius and let me look at it." And they brought one. And he said to them, "Whose likeness and inscription is this?" They said to him, "Caesar's." Jesus said to them, "Render to Caesar the things that are Caesar's, and to God the things that are God's." And they marveled at him. Mark 12:13-17

And another situation came about when Jesus was taken to Pilate to answer charges brought against by the Jewish leaders in Jerusalem.

When the chief priests and the guards saw him they cried out, "Crucify him, crucify him!" Pilate said to them, "Take him yourselves and crucify him. I find no guilt in him."

The Jews answered, "We have a law, and according to that law he ought to die, because he made himself the Son of God." Now when Pilate heard this statement, he became even more afraid, and went back into the praetorium and said to Jesus, "Where are you from?" Jesus did not answer him. So Pilate said to him, "Do you not speak to me? Do you not know that I have power to release you and I have power to crucify you?"

Jesus answered [him], "You would have no power over me if it had not been given to you from above. For this reason the one who handed me over to you has the greater sin."

This is quite a statement from the political leaders of the time. Are our politicians any better today? Some do not believe, but those are not the ones who worry me the most. Today's concerns are of the same source as the political concerns from 2,000 years ago. There are too many politicians that are try way too hard to prove that there are too many heretics out there, and those "heretics" are the cause of all of our problems We see in our society today! Jesus had a very important statement about this as well!

Hypocrite! First remove the plank from your own eye, and then you will see clearly to remove the speck from your brother's eye. Matthew 7:5

My Prayer: Oh, please Gracious Lord Jesus, help us clearly see the fault in our own observation and conclusions before we start laying blame at the feet of others. We do not demonstrate the unconditional love you give to us, and ask of us, when we accuse others yet do not recognize the impact of our own failed ways. We continuously ask for forgiveness knowing your grace will save us. However, how many times can we deny others the love you've commanded us to so readily and openly share with everyone, before your patience has been worn so thin. We are all, no matter what we claim or do not claim to be, in the same boat. Our only hope is that your patience exceeds our wildest expectation, and that you are, indeed, the most extraordinary example of Devine grace ever imagined. Please help all of us CHANGE! Those who read this devotion, those who don't, and especially those who believe they are more correct than any human has the right to believe they are. In that time from now until the order if God's Love is in place, we seek your grace and forgiveness! AMEN

Day 63

A Devotional for Understanding and Acceptance

What about feeling guilty? Should we have feelings of guilt if we have broken God's Laws?

Therefore, brothers, since we have confidence to enter the holy places by the blood of Jesus, by the new and living way that he opened for us through the curtain, that is, through his flesh, and since we have a great priest over the house of God, **let us draw near with a true heart in full assurance of faith, with our hearts sprinkled clean from an evil conscience and our bodies washed with pure water.** Hebrews 10:19-22

Paul gives us incredible hope in this statement. Why would we feel guilty if we have a TRUE HEART? If our heart is honed in on the commandment of Loving God with all our hearts, minds, soul, strength, and energy, we know we've been forgiven. And if we waiver, just renew your vow of faith to God, Savior, and the Spirit that binds us all together. You will be renewed in your forgiven state. Who among us is without sin. Who among us has resisted every temptation? Who among us has the power to forgive sins? Only ONE, and our goal is to seek AT-ONE-MENT with that gracious Savior!

Believing that your sins are forgiven means not feeling guilty beyond the attritional act of seeking forgiveness. Those who feel guilt have difficulty sharing the Good News, because the GOOD NEWS IS: Our Sins are Forgiven.

My Prayer: Gracious Lord Jesus, we thank you for the wonderful gift you've given us, the gift of Salvation. Help us remember that we've been freed of guilt the moment we ask you to forgive our wrong thinking and the behaviors those wrong thought generate. "And now these three remain: faith, hope and love. But the greatest of these is love." 1 Corinthians 13:13 AMEN

Day 64

A Devotional for Understanding and Acceptance

Isn't it enough that I pray before I eat and before I go to sleep at night?

Praying to give thanks for the meal we are going to eat and for safety and security as we sleep, is a good start. However, our life is actually a continuous prayer. If we believe we can hide anything at all from God, we truly do not know or understand the nature of our God. The consciousness of God is part of the consciousness that extends to, though, and beyond every part of our existence. Every person has experienced, at some level, even if they are not fully aware of the source of that experience, a connection to a source of power and energy that comes from Our Creator. If we can calm our thoughts and allow the experience to play out as far as possible, we might just have a life changing experience.

If we connect with the experience and acquire a real understanding of the nature of that experience, we will get closer to God. The more we quietly let God speak to us without saying a word, but just let God's Spirit connect with the spark that is within us, the closer we will get to the true Source of Life.

But the Advocate, the Holy Spirit, whom God will send in my name, will teach you all things and will remind you of everything I have said to you. Peace I leave with you; my peace I give you. I do not give to you as the world gives. Do not let your hearts be troubled and do not be afraid. John 14:26,27

You, however, are not in the realm of the flesh but are in the realm of the Spirit, if indeed the Spirit of God lives in you. And if anyone does not have the Spirit of Christ, they do not belong to Christ. Romans 8:9

My Prayer: Heavenly Creator God, help me quiet my mind and give me the patience to seek the Word as it is revealed in the connection between your spirit and the source of all, the spark that keeps my life on the path, as is written in the Gospels and in Paul's letter to the Church in Rome. We each have sensed your presence before and seek your continuous presence in our lives. Help us attend to your will focus as we conduct our lives. Thank you for loving us even when we are so unlovable! AMEN

Day 65

A Devotional for Understanding and Acceptance

If as Jesus stated: "I am the way and the truth and the life. No one comes to the Father except through me. John 14:6 Then why so many different denominations? Is each of these a different Path to Jesus? I don't have the definitive answer to this question, yet. I have asked that question myself during many of my meditative experiences and each time the answer that emerges is much simpler. The answer I come to is, each person will come to Jesus from where they are each day. Is a denomination, and its method of achieving a personal connection to Christ bringing you closer to the necessary relationship with Christ and the Holy Spirit, or is it a detour.

"You have heard the law that says, 'Love your neighbor and hate your enemy.' But I say, love your enemies! Pray for those who persecute you! In that way, you will be acting as true children of your Father in heaven. For he gives his sunlight to both the evil and the good, and he sends rain on the just and the unjust alike. If you love only those who love you, what reward is there for that? Even corrupt tax collectors do that much. If you are kind only to your friends, how are you different from anyone else? Even pagans do that. But you are to be perfect, even as your Father in heaven is perfect. Matthew 5:43-48 Remember, when Jesus was asked, what is the Greatest Commandment? His response was: "Jesus replied: 'Love the Lord your God with all your heart and with all your soul and with all your mind.' This is the first and greatest commandment. And the second is like it: 'Love your neighbor as yourself.' All the Law and the Prophets hang on these two commandments." Matthew 22: 37-40.

The answer I keep getting after years of meditation on the words of Christ; anyone who leads us away from those 2 commandments, is creating an unnecessary detour. If a detour has been placed in your way to Jesus, perhaps you should take a pause and seek a personal connection with Christ.

Hear our prayer oh Lord of Life and Creator God, please assist those who've been led astray or who've lost faith because of obstacles put in their way by unbending adherence to the letter of your commandment but huge failures to understand that the SPIRIT of those commandments requires that they be filtered through LOVE OF GOD AND LOVE OF OUR NEIGHBORS. Find a way, dear Jesus to retrieve those who've been chased from your Church by those who are too much like the Pharisee who prayed: "God, I thank you that I am not like other people—robbers, evildoers, adulterers—or even like this tax collector. I fast twice a week and give a tenth of all I get.'" But the tax collector stood at a distance.

He would not even look up to heaven, but beat his breast and said, "God, have mercy on me, a sinner." And Jesus said: "I tell you that this man, rather than the other, went home justified before God. For all those who exalt themselves will be humbled, and those who humble themselves will be exalted." Luke 18:9-14 Lord of Hosts, please help us bring all those rejected by the "too holy to care" back to you oh Great Holy Lord of all! AMEN!

Day 66

A Devotional for Understanding and Acceptance

Are you willing to take up your cross and follow Jesus?

What would that look like? Taking up our individual crosses, and then following Jesus! I'm convinced the Journey would be far different than 99% of What today's Christians think it is. My take in what Jesus asked us to do is speak truth to power, here in our communities, local churches, church organizational units, counties, states, and countries, as they exist today. We should be pointing out the acts that happen out of prejudice, inequality, corruption, self-serving-me-first priorities, and outright I don't love you and/or YOUR KIND behaviors. We should be examining the collective actions of each level of church governance as well as all political, business, and non-profit organizations.

Taking up his cross, our Savior was confronting these same issues that we are confronting today. The people of the world 2,000 years ago faced problems which have not changed. The technology has allowed to problems be magnified and the consequences of the wrong doings have geometrically increased due to multiple factors; such as advanced physical, emotional, and psychological weaponry being the most obvious. In his letter to the Galatians, the Apostle

Paul said: "But the fruit of the Spirit is love, joy, peace, forbearance, kindness, goodness, faithfulness, gentleness and self-control. Against such things there is no law." 5:22-23 The act of taking up our cross, even though doing so does treat others the way Christ and his disciples instructed us to, can put us in opposition to how mainstream society expects us to behave.

God our Creator and Jesus our Savior, please let your Spirit fall on our leaders so that they may see that our struggle is real. If we live in a very liberal area, our leaders often want to excuse all behaviors (except those behaviors exhibited by conservatives). This can result in citizens being subjected to unnecessary risks. If we live in a very conservative area, we may find that intolerance for all behaviors that leaders don't like and the related punishments can be extreme. Christ our Savior, you stated, let the one among you without sin cast the first stone, and no one stepped forward to start the stoning and that is where so many of our leaders fall short! Whose sins are worse? That's what I think you were asking. You were not saying, hey no big deal. Those guys were all sinners too, so go ahead and live your life any way you want. You said, "where are your accusers now? No one remains to condemn you, so neither will I. Go, and **SIN NO MORE!**" It's not that You we're saying it's ok to sin, You wants us all to examine our behaviors and repent, which means, in our hearts we know when we have behaved in a way that hurts others and either does not show our Love for God and/or Our Love for one another. Repentance means acknowledging when and how our behavior has harmed others and God, and then not continuing to live in a way that hurts God and hurts our neighbors. Somewhere between the 2 extremes there is reasonable alignment with turning away from SIN (behavior that shows disdain for our neighbors and/or God) and seeking forgiveness for the sins we've committed." Help us get beyond the extremes and need to free them all or seek retribution. **<u>AMEN</u>**

Day 67

A Devotional for Understanding and Acceptance

Can you believe what they are saying you must do to be on the good side with God?

Yes, I can believe it! It's a huge conspiracy! In fact, it's the biggest conspiracy of all time. A bunch of crazies are going around telling people, "You don't have to do anything!" In fact, they've gone as far as to say, "you can't do anything; because all mankind is flawed." They are saying and saying it out loud; "That's why Jesus came! To bridge the divide between mankind and our Amazing, Incredible Creator God!"

Who are these people? One guy's name was Simon but he changed his name to Peter. And another guy changed his name from Saul to Paul. And then there's James, and John, and then there's Thomas, Matthew, Phillip, Bartholomew, Simon and Matthias. There was also Judas but he ended up questioning things and thought he could force a change in direction. How can they all possibly believe that one man can pay the price of redemption for all. It's a conspiracy against Law and Order! Or is it?

The next day, the one after Preparation Day, the chief priests and the Pharisees went to Pilate. "Sir," they said, "we remember that while he was still alive that deceiver said, 'After three days I will rise again.' So give the order for the tomb to be made secure until the third day. Otherwise, his disciples may come and steal the body and tell the people that he has been raised from the dead. This last deception will be worse than the first." "Take a guard," Pilate answered. "Go, make the tomb as secure as you know how." So they went and made the tomb secure by putting a seal on the stone and posting the guard. (Matthew 27:62-66)

Am I Good Enough to get into Heaven?

For it is by grace you have been saved, through faith—and this (Salvation is) not from yourselves, it is the gift of God—not by works, so that no one can boast. (Ephesians 2:8,9)

Twenty-five years ago, German theologian Wolfhart Pannenberg told the magazine Prism:

"The evidence for Jesus' resurrection is so strong that nobody would question it except for two things: First, it is a very unusual event. And second, if you believe it happened, you have to change the way you live."

"Light has come into the world, but people loved darkness instead of light because their deeds were evil. Everyone who does evil hates the light, and will not come into the light for fear that their deeds will be exposed. But whoever lives by the truth comes into the light, so that it may be seen plainly that what they have done has been done in the sight of God."(John 3:19–21)

Gracious Creator God, please forgive us for our twisting of Jesus message. We have been told (and we Christians have all accepted that) we cannot ever be **a person good enough to get you into heaven!** Yet we too often point out that others must change, while ignoring our own need to change. Please forgive our continuing effort to usurp the power that only You and Your Son have the credentials to possess. We ask that you help us all remember: But many who are first will be last, and many who are last will be first. Matthew 19: 30 AMEN

Day 68

A Devotional for Understanding and Acceptance

What are we really looking for?

It seems to me that most people are looking for something that will create peace in their lives. No matter how much money, how many friends, how much they know, how powerful they become, most of us just aren't satisfied. Why is that? How much is enough?

The LORD will keep you from all harm - he will watch over your life; the LORD will watch over your coming and going both now and forevermore. Psalm 121:7-8

There will never be enough money, things, friends, power, or anything to satisfy any of us. The only peace we can truly find will be in our own hearts as our hearts are In dwelled by the Spirit of the Living God! I know I struggle. It seems that I feel my life is going along just fine! I feel like it's all under control and then, I start thinking oh wouldn't it be so much better if only…… And then WHAM! It's back to reality. Oh that I could put aside my constant wanting, which I usually interpret as NEEDING! I am in need of so little. But I want so much!

For the time will come when people will not tolerate sound doctrine and accurate instruction [that challenges them with God's truth]; but wanting to have their ears tickled [with something pleasing], they will accumulate for themselves [many] teachers [one after another, chosen] to satisfy their own desires and to support the errors they hold. 2 Timothy 4:3 This truth holds for both those who want to severely control people and what they think and do, and for those who want to be free to do anything they want, all the time.

Somewhere between the Libertines (those who say anything goes) and the strictest disciplinarians, there exists the Love of Christ. Both extremes hate either God or humans or both. "Whoever claims to love God yet hates a brother or sister is a liar. For whoever does not love their brother and sister, whom they have seen, cannot love God, whom they have not seen." 1John 4:20

Savior Jesus and the Parental God of all, hear our prayer! We all truly want to have that faith that leaves everything and everyone in your care. Help ease our struggle and let us become one with your will through the spirit you sent to watch over us. It is difficult but we realize it is only difficult because we want to be in charge! We want to control our lives and every other thing that can impact our lives. Help us to seek your peace and an understanding of how our world really works. Bless this day and the gifts you have given us! For it is through gratitude that we begin to open up to the Devine within us! AMEN

Day 69

A Devotional for Understanding and Acceptance

Have you ever been asked: how can you be so relaxed when everything is going crazy all around you?

The Culture Wars are not real! They are contrived to separate us based on fear. Here's an example: Many years ago, my job wasn't going well and it seemed like I had just picked the wrong career. I even went through a career renewal and future career research program in Chicago. I took an assessment and went to a series of seminars. In the end, a counselor said, "based on your assessment and all the workshop participation, it's not your career that's wrong, it's the school district you are working for. Change districts! Find a school system with values aligned with you and your level of satisfaction and happiness will be greatly improved!" Once I accepted that I had to leave, I became much more relaxed and calmer.

"Who is going to harm you if you are eager to do good? But even if you should suffer for what is right, you are blessed. "Do not fear their threats; do not be frightened." But in your hearts revere Christ as Lord. Always be prepared to give an answer to everyone who asks you to give the reason for the hope that you have. But do this with gentleness and respect, keeping a clear conscience, so that those who speak maliciously against your good behavior in Christ may be ashamed of their slander."

1 Peter 3:13-16

After this realization was made clear and I accepted it, one of the best teachers in that school, a teacher revered by students, staff, and parents alike, asked me the question at the beginning of this devotional. The answer I gave surprised even me! I simply said to her, "once it became clear that no one could drain my soul of the spirit Christ put there, everything else just became far less important. And I read the quote above from 1st Peter chapter 3.

After 24 years, the very same district sought my help to get the district back on track. I decided to help and didn't always agree 100% with everything the school board wanted to do and explained to them why we had a difference of opinion and we moved forward. But we never went after each other in an extremely negative way. We could all agree that we had the same ultimate goal in mind. And we decided to present information to students and allow them to come to their own conclusions. We decided we would present both sides of each story so that they had exposure to as much as we knew and together families could decide.

My Prayer: Heavenly Gracious Creator God, You created us and allowed us to learn, grown, develop, and contribute to our world.

Every single one of us who has ever tread on this planet has contributed, in one way or another, to the world as we experience it today. And each deserves to have their part of the story told. Let us stop bickering and tell the whole story. We ask this be done in the name of the one who has shown his love for all, Jesus Christ. AMEN

Day 70

A Devotional for Understanding and Acceptance

Where has violence taken us over the Centuries? And could a non-violent approach change the world?

And he said to them, When I sent you out without money or bag or shoes, were you in need of anything? And they said, Nothing. And he said to them, But now, he who has a money-bag, or a bag for food, let him take it: and he who has not, let him give his coat for money and get a sword.

Luke 25:35-36. Does this mean that Jesus was expecting his disciples to respond to violent, aggressive behaviors with their own acts of violence? If that was the case, why did Jesus do this?

When those around him recognized what was about to happen, they said, "Lord, should we fight with our swords?" One of them struck the high priest's servant, cutting off his right ear. Jesus responded, "Stop! No more of this!" He touched the slave's ear and healed him.

Like 22: 49-51 So, if Jesus refused to let his disciples protect him with their swords, why did he say what he did in verses 35 & 36? Some biblical scholars have suggested that Jesus was, indeed egging his followers on to violence, but that just seems out of character based on the rest of what Jesus says in throughout the Gospels and the way the Apostles lived from the Resurrection until their deaths.

Paul tells us in his letter to the Church at Ephesus: "So he came and proclaimed peace to you who were far off and peace to those who were near; for through him both of us have access in one Spirit to the Father." Ephesians 2:17,18

"Blessed are the peacemakers, for they will be called children of God" Matthew 5:9

Those that would try to convince that Jesus wanted Violent Retribution for the acts of those who denied his divinity, don't quite understand the power and might of God. Any God who must spread the Word by force, isn't really The God after all. No one worth Our God's attention, would make decisions, on the basis of fear! Fear is a very low grade emotion and requires nothing other than avoidance. On the other hand, Our Awesome God attracts people with the promise of life without pain and suffering. Life based on loving kindness and the true strength that stems from caring faith and commitment.

Gracious God, thank you for ensuring that your Message is spread with Love and that you seek love, faith and commitment from us rather than fear and trepidation. Through the ages, so many people, who truly do not know or understand God, have tried to force people to accept and revere God. As has been the case in so many situations and circumstances in the past, fear of pain and suffering can produce minimal compliance but fall short on inspiring love and devotion from people. We praise your wisdom and are eternally grateful for your acceptance. Help us fulfill your will and through our love of You, love for our fellow humans, and by leading people to discipleship and your salvation, let us be all that you desire for us! AMEN

Day 71

A Devotional for Understanding and Acceptance

Did Jesus really want to accept all people into the faith? What about prostitutes, pimps, drug dealers, murderers, and even Moslems, Buddhists, Agnostics, pop and Atheists? If he were to be assigned a church to pastor in 2023, what would his congregation look like?pp

Let's look at his record: Jesus accepted the following people:

- women who had committed adultery

- a man who was convicted as a thief

- a tax collector (they did not always/usually conduct themselves in an honest and honorable manner

- a homeless man who lived in a cave and by all descriptions was either epileptic or mentally ill or both

- a Roman Centurion

- several "unclean" people with skin lesions and other diseases

- poor and helpless people

- widows and orphans

- paralytic, blind, deaf, and uneducated people, Samaritans

- or anyone who most of us would reject today

Ok, so you show up to church next Sunday morning, and the minister begins the service with an introduction of new members: the pastor starts off with a few women: "first, I'd like to have you meet this Hannah, a widow who has very little to financially contribute but she will give what she can.

Next, there is Sarah, she was a drug addicted prostitute, she's had a really rough time but she has been waiting for an opportunity to be forgiven and truly wants to change. The third new member is Frank, a government worker who ran into some difficulty and made some poor decisions, he did his time for those poor decisions and wants to start a fresh. Our fourth new member was a member of a foreign military unit and fought against US interests, but he asks that he get a fresh start. Bob had a terrible contagious disease, and Shannon couldn't read or write! The Harold family, all 7 of them, have been homeless for 18 months and will be sleeping at night in our fellowship hall until we can help them find room in the community housing for the homeless center. These 13 new members are just beginning next week, we will bring 8 more new members in and the week after, I have 11 more. In just 3 weeks, our little congregation will increase our membership by more than 20%. Our congregation will grow from 155 members to 187 in just a few weeks. God has blessed us!

Tell me, truthfully. How excited are you to have these 32 new members in your church?

Gracious Glorious Savior, help us remember why you came to us as the Messiah. You did not come to make the wealthy, richer; or to make those in power, more powerful; or the healthy, healthier; or the beautiful, more beautiful, or to give those with food even more food! Awesome God let all your children enjoy your blessings! We should be honored that our church is following your Great Commission. If we were so fortunate to have these 32 new members—we'd be doing our part to make disciples of the all the world! AMEN

Day 72

A Devotional for Understanding and Acceptance

Is it a matter of just outlasting all the rest?

There are a number of survivor type TV shows on these days! Last night I watched a few interesting episodes of one called "Outlast" pits 4 teams of 4 members against one another in the cold, wet Alaskan Wilderness. Another called "Alone," requires individuals to survive without contact with other people and with minimal supplies. Of course, there's the network TV show, Survivor, which involves treachery, deceit, and provides incentives to encourage competition.

Our salvation is not a competition and not about being the lone survivor. It's about helping as many people as possible acquire the ultimate tool box for a thriving community based on God's saving grace in the person of Jesus Christ. There are places in our world that live in the loving harmony of Jesus. It doesn't have to be a commune. It just needs to be a truly loving system where people commit to an ideal of, no one will be left uncared for.

For you were called to freedom, brothers and sisters; only do not use your freedom as an opportunity for self-indulgence, but through love become willing helpers to one another. For the whole law is summed up in a single commandment, "You shall love your neighbor as yourself."

(Galatians 5:13-14)

[F]or in Christ Jesus you are all children of God through faith. As many of you as were baptized into Christ have clothed yourselves with Christ. There is no longer Jew or Greek, there is no longer slave or free, there is no longer male and female; for all of you are one in Christ Jesus.

(Galatians 3:26-28)

In these two passages, it certainly does not appear that the Apostle Paul, (a renowned persecutor of the followers of Jesus who was converted as it is reported in Chapter 9 of the Book of Acts, and definitely someone who believed only God's chosen people deserved to be cared for) thought as he wrote to the Church in Galatia, that it's not ok to feather your own nest and ignore others who go without. Furthermore, no one is better than any other. We are all equal in the eyes of God!

Hear our Prayer Lord Jesus and Creator God of All; help us overcome our personal insistence that **WE ARE RIGHT** and all those who think differently must be wrong. Lord, please help us realize that, if we are in the Leadership position, it is incumbent upon us to find the critical common pieces that do exist, and then make certain that those agreements become the cornerstone of positive path forward. Help us us understand that it's neither a sprint nor a marathon; the road to salvation is a point in time! For God so loved the world that he gave his one and only Son, that whoever believes in him shall not perish but have eternal life. (John 3:16) That's already done for you; now comes your point in time, just accept it and believe it! AMEN

Day 73

A Devotional for Understanding and Acceptance

When do the tough really get going?

Do you remember the old saying, when the going gets tough, the tough get going? In order to understand the true meaning of that platitude, we have to clarify a couple of concepts. First, how tough is it when the going is considered the point at which the tough will get going? Another consideration, is the situation ever so "tough" that, even though the tough are getting their behinds in gear, they lack the power to significantly change the course of events? Perhaps toughness is a relative term. It's entirely possible for individuals to have differing degrees of toughness. Some of us have marshmallow bodies and marshmallow intensities of focus, drive, and grit. And then there are those among us with bodies seemingly made of granite and intensities with the resolve of titanium steel, laser focused, and with enough grit to file a bed of nails into a comfortable mattress.

Unfortunately, Iron Man and all of the DC and Marvel Comic fictional Super Heroes, are just that FICTION! The only human ever to overcome the power unleashed by the creative-yet-incredibly-destructive forces of man's own greed and hunger for power and control, was a man who refused to exert his overwhelming power, focus, and grit. Instead he chose to show Mercy and Love and Peace and Joy! "Greater love has no one than this: to lay down one's life for one's friends." John 15:13

How many people would you lay down your life for? 10, 20, perhaps 100? Jesus laid down his life for everyone who has ever lived, everyone who is a live at this very moment, and everyone who will ever live. The skeptics might say, once you're dead, you might as well say he died for everyone. But Jesus has risen again from the dead. He has mastered death, overcome the destruction to the body death causes. He opens the passage for everyone. We can have the same experience. We simply must knock, and the door will be opened for us! We simply must ask and we will receive. "Ask and it will be given to you; seek and you will find; knock and the door will be opened to you." Matthew 7:7

Gracious Jesus, thank you for going to the Cross and giving your life just for me! I realize that you've given everyone who believes in you, that same right to make that same claim! That's the beauty of your salvation. All who accept you are a friend for whom you laid down your life. That's fairly easy to comprehend and accept. The incredible, amazing thing is that you also, personally laid down your life for millions of people who do not believe, simply on the HOPE that each one will be illuminated, and through that enlightenment, achieve atonement and unite with your spirit. To completely enjoy the totality of eternal life, we must have complete acceptance and open our hearts and spirits which will then allow our minds to fully understand. We cannot reason our way to a connection with you oh lord, for our capacity for logic is insufficient to grasp the complete picture. The pathway is not logic, it's **LOVE! AMEN**

Day 74

A Devotional for Understanding and Acceptance

What do you do when the carry out dinner you just ordered, is ready before the cup of Tea, you ordered to drink while you wait for your carryout order to be prepared? I think it's time to practice my patience and to be a gracious customer. The following three versus are quite clear. Our role as Christian's is never to be heavy handed. Our purpose is love!

"Better to be patient than a warrior, and better to have self-control than to capture a city." Proverbs 16:32

"We who are powerful need to be patient with the weakness of those who don't have power, and not (just react to) please ourselves" Romans 15:1

"But this is why I was shown mercy, so that Christ Jesus could show his endless patience to me first of all. So I'm an example for those who are going to believe in him for eternal life." 1 Timothy 1:16

"But the fruit of the Spirit is love, joy, peace, patience, kindness, goodness, faithfulness, gentleness, and self-control..." Galatians 5:22-23

Glorious, Gracious, Creator, hear our prayer; your divine nature is to love and encourage us. We realize that our lives are a gift of time that to you is but an instant, yet each moment can seem so precious; so, in our attempt to get all that we can out of our lives, we become impatient. Help us use each of these events as an opportunity to allow the world around us to slow down. Help us realize, that no matter how fast we try to complete our daily journey, there's more going on than just what we see before our own eyes. As the Apostle Paul has told us: "Preach the word. Be ready to do it whether it is convenient or inconvenient. Correct, confront, and encourage with **'Patience'** and instruction." 2 Timothy 4:2

Be with us in our comings and goings; while we hurry and while we patiently wait; when we are anxious and calm; when we are despondent and when we are full of hope! For there is no greater Goal than arrive into your presence side by side with our Diverse, Loving Choir of Equals! It is so marvelous to know, all are included in your invitation to join your heavenly Chorus! AMEN

Day 75

A Devotional for Understanding and Acceptance

What does it mean when we say that's permanent?

If something is permanent, is that the same as being eternal? We might say that a steel rod, that is 20 feet long, and driven into the ground and then encased in a cylinder of 12 in diameter and 5 feet thick of hardened concrete. It would seem that the steel rod's placement in the ground is intended to be permanent. However, the steel rod will rust and be effected and react with chemicals in the environment. If we think this is an eternal reality for the steel rod, I can assure you, some atoms in that rod will be exchanged for other atoms, and the fundamental nature of that rod will alter with time. I would argue that permanent May be a long-long-long time; but it is not eternal; not forever and ever and ever.

In the world of physics, we've gone through several iterations of our understanding of what is temporary and what is permanent. At one point we thought matter can neither be created nor destroyed. Then, Einstein's Theory of Relativity ushered in the Nuclear Energy concept and new matter was created, atoms were changed in structure and matter was converted into energy, thus matter was destroyed and created. Next came Quantum Mechanics and we understood that matter and energy we actually just different expressions of existence.

The more we learn, the more we need God to help us explain and understand. In fact, nothing makes sense without an eternal consciousness that has the capacity to create something out of nothing! The latest images from our telescopes in space suggest that everything we thought we knew about our universe may be wrong and perhaps the very concept of (Uni)verse needs to be rethought.

Are you confused yet? It seems the more we think we've got it all figured out, the more we realize we know and understand so little. God's nature and presence is revealed to us when we realize that in the context of the enormity of everything, we appear to be nearly nothing, but in the context of totality of nothingness we appear to be almost everything.

Emanuel—God with us: Jesus, son of Man/Son of God. It is natural for us to praise you and seek your company. It is natural for us to wonder and ask questions. It is natural for us to think physical when we should stop thinking and start opening our emotional connection from our hearts to the Heart of the Living God! We are so insignificant in the proportion of matter that we occupy in all that exists, yet you have sought us out to connect with. You know me, and all my brothers and sisters, better than we know ourselves. We pray that we will, through our individual awareness, truly appreciate, know, and understand how fortunate we are. Thank you Lord God for everything we are, we have, and all we can ever be. AMEN

Day 76

A Devotional for Understanding and Acceptance

Are you a Saint? What does it take to be a Saint?

To be a saint means you have been sanctified. Set apart from the world to be a true witness to the power and glory of God and the Savior, Christ Jesus. The Apostle Paul explains how the Gentiles became Sanctified in his letter to the Church in Rome.

Through him we received grace and apostleship to call all the Gentiles to the obedience that comes from faith for his name's sake. And you also are among those Gentiles who are called to belong to Jesus Christ. To all in Rome who are loved by God and called to be his holy people: Grace and peace to you from God our Father and from the Lord Jesus Christ.

First, I thank my God through Jesus Christ for all of you, because your faith is being reported all over the world.

God, whom I serve in my spirit in preaching the gospel of his Son, is my witness how constantly I remember you. Roman 1:5-9

Being a Saint does not mean being perfect! Only Christ was perfect. Being devoted to the perfection of Christ and his purpose is the primary requirement of being a Saint. Miracles happen everyday. But, in order for any miraculous event to occur the person benefitting from the miracle must have enormous faith in the positive potential for the miraculous outcome. It is God's will being done when it appeared that there was no hope of that outcome.

There are tremendous arguments made for the logical disbelief of miracles happening. Most of these logical arguments are based on the work of David Hume, who believed that in order for a miracle to occur, an outcome must violate natural law. On the other hand Hume believed that natural law was violable! At the time, the primary belief was that Newtonian Physics established the parameters of Natural Law. Since the 1700's we have witnessed Newtonian Physics being miraculously altered. The discovery of quantum physics has created real proof of forces that cannot be explained through Newtonian physics and these forces have led to amazing astrophysics discoveries and the ushering in of nuclear power and quantum mechanics.

Miracles happen every day, if we will only look for them! Why does one person have a stage four, go home and prepare to die prognosis of pancreatic cancer get cured in short order, while another person with an identical disease and an identical prognosis, succumbs to the disease and meets the doctors predicted end.

Take a look at this example, provided by Lee Strobel, the investigative reporter for the Chicago Tribune who blue the whistle on the Ford Motor Company and the deadly fires happening in the Pinto!

Barbara Snyder was diagnosed at the Mayo Clinic with multiple sclerosis. She deteriorated over a period of many years, several operations, many hospitalizations," Strobel explained. "It got to the point where she was dying. And, in fact, one doctor described her as being one of the most hopelessly ill patients he'd ever encountered."

One day, one of her friends called WMBI, which is the radio station in Chicago run by the Moody Bible Institute, and said, 'Pray for Barbara. She's on her deathbed,'" Strobel explained. "So, we know that at least 450 Christians began praying for her, because they wrote letters saying, 'We're praying for you.'"

This male voice coming from the corner of the room where nobody was, said, 'Get up my child and walk,'" Strobel recounted. "So she basically pulls the tube out of her throat, says, 'Go find my parents'

[and] jumps out of bed."

Gracious God, we all know of someone in need of healing. Let our prayers rise up to you and may those in need be healed. We believe in your miraculous healing power. Please dear God, heal ______, whom we truly care about today. AMEN

Please put the name of someone who needs healing in the blank!

Day 77

A Devotional for Understanding and Acceptance

What can we learn from "March Madness" that can help us build a stronger faith?

So many athletic teams have some very outwardly noticeable members of the team that give credit to God for their success. I'm not certain that their success is due to divine intervention, but certainly the talent they develop has been influenced by God's gifts. But in most contests, both sides have athletes blessed with talent. With so many other issues in the world that should take precedence over sports championships, it seems likely that Our Savior would be much more interested in the good that we do for the least of these than whether UCLA, Ohio State, Alabama, Duke, Kansas or UNC are crowned NCAA Champions. Our Savior is, most likely, more interested in how we use the blessings we've been entrusted with to further the cause of creating more disciples and empowering more people to improve their lives and relationship with God.

So no matter who you hope brings home the NCAA Basketball Trophy (Men's or Women's) remember, it's not the talent that will make the difference. It's how they use their talent in pursuit of greater equity, and inclusivity of all people in God's wonderful plan that is most important.

For just as the body is one and has many members, and all the members of the body, though many, are one body, so it is with Christ. For in one Spirit we were all baptized into one body—Jews or Greeks, slaves or free—and all were made to drink of one Spirit. For the body does not consist of one member but of many. If the foot should say, "Because I am not a hand, I do not belong to the body," that would not make it any less a part of the body. And if the ear should say, "Because I am not an eye, I do not belong to the body," that would not make it any less a part of the body. .1 Corinthians: 12:12-27

My brothers, show no partiality as you hold the faith in our Lord Jesus Christ, the Lord of glory. For if a man wearing a gold ring and fine clothing comes into your assembly, and a poor man in shabby clothing also comes in, and if you pay attention to the one who wears the fine clothing and say, "You sit here in a good place," while you say to the poor man, "You stand over there," or, "Sit down at my feet," have you not then made distinctions among yourselves and become judges with evil thoughts? James 2:1-4

Heavenly, Gracious, Creator Lord; help us remember why you provided us with talent and opportunities for us to excel at using those talents, not for our own edification and glory, but to be better capable of Glorifying your creation and your name. Help us also remember that it is in help our brothers and sisters succeed that we achieve our highest potential as your children. When all of God's creation is cared for, we all win! AMEN

Day 78

A Devotional for Understanding and Acceptance

How can you turn a very necessary task, which you do not like, into an enlightening experience that leaves you more enthusiastic about life than ever before?

Sound like a pipe dream? Jesus explained this so many times, yet we ignore this part of his teaching! The answer is in why we do what we do. Consider this situation. We do not to offend people and drive them away from salvation but we also need to sit at the foot of our savior.

As Jesus and his disciples were on their way, he came to a village where a woman named Martha opened her home to him. She had a sister called Mary, who sat at the Lord's feet listening to what he said. But Martha was distracted by all the preparations that had to be made. She came to him and asked, "Lord, don't you care that my sister has left me to do the work by myself? Tell her to help me!"

"Martha, Martha," the Lord answered, "you are worried and upset about many things, but few things are needed—or indeed only one. Mary has chosen what is better, and it will not be taken away from her." Luke 10:38-42

"All authority in heaven and on earth has been given to me. Therefore go and make disciples of all nations, baptizing them in the name of the Father and of the Son and of the Holy Spirit, and teaching them to obey everything I have commanded you. And surely I am with you always, to the very end of the age." Matthew 28:18-20

We must take time for instruction yet still take care of more mundane tasks. In those tasks we can see the importance they gave to God if we will only look at each task as a way to maintain the beauty of God's Creation. As you go through your daily tasks, do not put yourself on autopilot. Remain aware of everything involved in completing each part of the task. For it is in the attention to detail that we acquire a true appreciation for the magnificence of our Creator. The Creator knew, before he engaged in the act of Creation what would be required to keep the totality of Creation as wonderful and marvelous as it is.

Amazing Creator God, we pray to you that we would never take your creation for granted. It is the detail of creation that shows the extraordinarily amazing qualities of being alive. Help us maintain our focus so that we can never even think of allowing any part of this beautiful creation to be destroyed. Help us never be guilty of just going through the motions. It is in appreciating your work that we begin to understand your power, might, and glory.

Help us maintain our awareness and consciousness in our daily work. If we should sleepwalk through this life, we run a terrible risk of missing opportunities to glorify Your Name. AMEN

Day 79

A Devotional for Understanding and Acceptance

What's the big deal with the first day of spring?

Today, we hit the Vernal Equinox. That point in the year when the number of hours of daylight is almost the same as the number of hours of darkness. It's that point when the sun is directly overhead at 12:00 noon at the equator. It's that point when we all know that winter is behind us (if we live north of the Tropic of Cancer, which is 23.5 degrees north longitude. For those of us living more in the 38 degree to 45 degree north, or more temperate zones of the Northern Hemisphere, it means we're moving out of the dark and into the light.

So this is one of those amazing God things! If the Earth had been created without a tilted axis, life as we know it would not exist. It is the periods of time when there is little sunlight that allow the environment to rest and the differential in atmospherics temperatures that allow the weather patterns to do what they do! It's not an accident, it's absolutely necessary.

Everything about our Earth and the other bodies in our solar system create the optimal circumstances for life as we know it. The size of our Sun, the distance our Earth is from the Sun, the axial tilt, the rotational velocity of our planet as well as its orbital velocity, and the size of the remaining planets in this solar system: all of this make life not only possible but quite probable. There may be other solar systems that meet all these same criteria, but we do not know for certainty that another perfect system exists.

Could all this happen by mere chance? Yes, to say others would be to say we know, without a doubt, exactly how God created our world. That would be folly and would demonstrate a hubristic attitude on our part. By chance or specific design doesn't really matter. The critical concept is don't stop doing our critical investigations and analysis. That is how we can assure we are not the cause of our ultimate demise.

And through him to reconcile to himself all things, whether on earth or in heaven, making peace by the blood of his cross. Colossians 1:20

Put on then, as God's chosen ones, holy and beloved, compassionate hearts, kindness, humility, meekness, and patience, Colossians 3:12

But if anyone has the world's goods and sees his brother in need, yet closes his heart against him, how does God's love abide in him? Little children, let us not love in word or talk but in deed and in truth. 1 John 3:17-18

Gracious Lord Jesus, forgive our short sightedness. We think we know and we behave as if we were the creator. But, we get it wrong time and time again. Your creation is so perfect. Our job must be to care for it with a heart that is as pure as was God's when it was created. Lead us to a more beautiful understanding of how to care for your creation. If our ineptitude should jeopardize this marvelous creation, teach us what we must do to restore the home you granted us, if it is possible to do so. AMEN

Day 80

A Devotional for Understanding and Acceptance

How can overcome exactly what I am, and be what God's purpose is for me?

Let's answer that question with another question. How do you know that what you are is not exactly what God's purpose is for you? Is it because it's too uncomfortable trying to go against the flow? Or is it because you're afraid that if you fulfill your purpose, people will think you're a goody two shoes or something like that?

In a recent conversation with a business leader, the leader commented that he was a pessimist. I asked him why he said that. His response was, if he's responsible for a project he looks for what could go wrong, plans for how to keep the bad things from happening, and then proceeds. I told him, you are not pessimistic, you are a planner. A pessimist says, that will never work, whereas, a planner tries to anticipate potential problems and creates plans to prevent them from happening. Every team needs a great planner. Otherwise, the unanticipated potholes can ruin the vehicle you are depending on to achieve the desired outcome.

Now, you can be a pessimistic planner; the individual that not only looks for the potholes but then uses them as an excuse for abandoning important work. Or you can be an optimistic planner; the individual that looks for the potholes and then makes plans for either circumventing the potholes or fix the potholes. Then it's move forward toward the achievement of the objective. There are 2 other types though. There are saboteurs; those people who hate change/progress and do everything they can to make every change result in catastrophe. The second is the anchor. No matter what, the anchor tries to keep the organization from moving in any direction at all. The saboteurs act in the basis of change makes me feel anxious and anxiety equals unhappiness; therefore, if I'm not happy, no one's going to be happy! The anchor's goal is to let everyone know, happiness is not in the cards but at least we can be content in our present state.

"Therefore, if anyone is in Christ, the new creation has come: The old has gone, the new is here!" 2 Peter 2:9

"Therefore, I urge you, brothers and sisters, in view of God's mercy, to offer your bodies as a living sacrifice, holy and pleasing to God—this is your true and proper worship. Do not conform to the pattern of this world, but be transformed by the renewing of your mind. Then you will be able to test and approve what God's will is—his good, pleasing and perfect will." Romans 12:1-2

And he (Jesus) said: "Truly I tell you, unless you change and become like little children, you will never enter the kingdom of heaven. Matthew 18:3

Of all humans, we know that children will definitely change. They learn, understand, figure out how to solve problems, and grow in stature, strength, and hopefully, faith.

Gracious Creator God, thank you for helping us see that there is no true faith without change. If we are to undergo transformational change, please let us become closer and closer to you and let us gain greater understanding of what is expected of us. Help us find the potholes in our path before our lives become seriously and irreparably injured. Be our guide through this life and help us change course as needed. Please help us make sure that any alterations we go through, happen because the changes will bring us closer to our purpose. We offer prayers for all who struggle with the potholes, roadblocks, and setbacks. Whether it is health, finances, or faith, we know that our Redeemer can alleviate our misery. Lead us into your healing presence and give us a heart full of love and grace. AMEN

Day 81

A Devotional for Understanding and Acceptance

On March 22, 1942 Sir Stanford Cripps, a British Statesman went to India to negotiate with Mahatma Gandhi, the Leader of the Independence Movement in India, to seek their support in the war effort. They were willing to negotiate independence for the nearly one billion people in India in order to gain their support for the war effort against fascism in Europe and the aggression by Japan in Asia. Gandhi was definitely in favor of opposing both of the forces opposing Great Britain but he could not guarantee that all his fellow Indians seeking independence would feel the same. So he could not guarantee that all Indian military would support the Allies during WWII.

After the end of WWII, it took 2 more years before India gained its independence. Some might say, if they only had openly supported the Allies they would have gained independence sooner. What if the Colonies had just been good partners with Great Britain? Could we have gained our independence without a war? Why should anyone have to fight to be FREE!

You, my brothers and sisters, were called to be free. But do not use your freedom to indulge the flesh ; rather, serve one another humbly in love.

For the entire law is fulfilled in keeping this one command: "Love your neighbor as yourself." Galatians 5:13-14

Perhaps, we should all heed this ancient advice from Proverbs 10:9. "Whoever walks in integrity walks securely, but he who makes his ways crooked will be found out."

And the Jesus is quoted in Luke 6: 32-42:

"If you love those who love you, what benefit is that to you? For even sinners love those who love them. And if you do good to those who do good to you, what benefit is that to you? For even sinners do the same. And if you lend to those from whom you expect to receive, what credit is that to you? Even sinners lend to sinners, to get back the same amount. But love your enemies, and do good, and lend, expecting nothing in return, and your reward will be great, and you will be sons of the Most High, for he is kind to the ungrateful and the evil. Be merciful, even as your Father is merciful."

Heavenly Gracious God, teach us the difference between serving our fellow humans from a place of humility and love and the many ways we try to demonstrate a very hollow kindness as a tool for furthering our own agenda. For centuries, our history has reported the best of the victors and ignored the plight of the vanquished. Help us remember that our desires for property and wealth do not negate the rights of others to continue to exist and thrive. We should not be angry with those who do not willingly give up their way of life just so that we can assuage our own guilt for past transgressions. The victors do get to write their own version of history, however do not be fooled; because you write history, does not make your version the correct version. Gracious Lory Jesus, as we enter this Holiest of all seasons; once again we ask for your forgiveness. Our sins are many, and perhaps this time, as each of us enumerates our own sins, we will truly beg for your forgiveness and turn away from these behaviors and **CHANGE! AMEN**

Day 82

A Devotional for Understanding and Acceptance

How aware are you of everything that is going on around you? I have been looking at my personal mindfulness and I've come to some interesting conclusions.

First of all, I have always thought of my life experiences as events that happen and I either recognize my role in them or I feel like I was just an observer without a role. This was the very first misconception that I realized I had complete wrong. If I recognize an event as having taken place, I have some connection to that event. No matter how minor my involvement in the event, the only events that I truly become aware of are events that either have a positive or a negative impact on what I believe I am. I cannot deny it's existence, nor can I suppress my experience if it. To say that something does not concern you, and you are aware of it, is to tell a horrible lie to yourself and everyone else.

Watch your life and doctrine closely. Persevere in them, because if you do, you will save both yourself and your hearers.

1 Timothy 4:16

God knows everything about you and Loves you anyway! We truly cannot believe we can deny any aspect of his creation as being crucial in his eyes, can we?

Gracious God, forgive our feeble attempts at saying, this or that does not concern me. Remind us that all of your creation, every rock, every tree, every animal, every person, and all that exists is precious to you and we are responsible for its care. Help us have the strength to be the human beings you've designed us to be. Fully aware, fully responsible, fully awake, and most importantly fully ALIVE! AMEN!

Day 83

A Devotional for Understanding and Acceptance

How much should we count on others to come to our assistance?

Ideally, there should no question as to whether or not we should be able to count on others in our time of need. However, too many people never got the message. Those that truly went above and beyond even the wildest expectations of the most down and out of humanity, the mother Theresas, the Gandhis, the Mandalas, and others heard, accepted, and delivered on the message. But it appears that those who think otherwise are in a very big majority.

When did we see you sick or in prison and go to visit you?' "The King will reply, 'Truly I tell you, whatever you did for one of the least of these brothers and sisters of mine, you did for me.' Matthew 25:39-41

"A righteous man knows the rights of the poor; a wicked man does not understand such knowledge." Proverbs 29:7

"Give, and it will be given to you. A good measure, pressed down, shaken together and running over, will be poured into your lap. For with the measure you use, it will be measured to you." Luke 6:28

Since Christ was quite clear in what he deemed to be the most important commandments; Love God with all your heart, mind, strength and soul; and Love your neighbor as I have loved you. With these notions, laid out with Crystal Clarity, how can anyone not care, and care with the compassion Christ demands of us, for every human being. The answer to the question absolutely should be, though it doesn't appear to be the reality today!

Gracious Redeemer: our Salvation, Comfort, and Hope, please help us get beyond our own selfish, narrow mindedness, and help us realize that we will be rewarded in our life everlasting based on our willingness to give of our own resources to make sure others have what they will need to secure a more positive future. Thank you for loving me as much as you do and for providing for our continued success. All of this we pray to you in the name of our Holy Creator God. We know we should care more but we are stuck in a cycle of belief that looks at our world not from an attitude of Abundance, but from the position of limitations and struggle. We know we can do better, please help us discover our better selves. In the name of our God and Savior we pray for support and guidance! AMEN

Day 84

A Devotional for Understanding and Acceptance

When you are having a bad series of days, do you find yourself saying: "Why is this happening to me?"

There are many who believe that they are being wrongfully treated or even punished because of things that are happening beyond their control. However, most events in our life happen because of where our thoughts take us. As we look at the world around us, the more negatives we see, the more negatives we continue to experience. Consider how we view the most downtrodden and destitute of our society through the lens Jesus provides. When you read these verses read them first thinking of each person as the people you see every day committing crimes, being drunk on the sidewalk downtown, or just panhandling at a major intersection.

"Then he will say to those on his left, 'Depart from me, you who are cursed, into the eternal fire prepared for the devil and his angels. For I was hungry, and you gave me nothing to eat, I was thirsty, and you gave me nothing to drink, I was a stranger and you did not invite me in, I needed clothes and you did not clothe me, I was sick and in prison and you did not look after me.' They also will answer, 'Lord, when did we see you hungry or thirsty or a stranger or needing clothes or sick or in prison, and did not help you?' He will reply, 'Truly I tell you, whatever you did not do for one of the least of these, you did not do for me.' Then they will go away to eternal punishment, but the righteous to eternal life." Matthew 25:41-46

Now re-read the verses from the point of view that each of those you've seen were dearly loved relatives and friends just going through a rough spot in their lives. Will your response to these people result in a different response from the king? Then the King will say to those on his right, 'Come, you who are blessed by my Father; take your inheritance, the kingdom prepared for you since the creation of the world. For I was hungry, and you gave me something to eat, I was thirsty, and you gave me something to drink, I was a stranger and you invited me in, I needed clothes, and you clothed me, I was sick and you looked after me, I was in prison and you came to visit me.' Then the righteous will answer him, 'Lord, when did we see you hungry and feed you, or thirsty and give you something to drink? When did we see you as a stranger and invite you in, or needing clothes and clothe you? When did we see you sick or in prison and go to visit you?' The King will reply, 'Truly I tell you, whatever you did for one of the least of these brothers and sisters of mine, you did for me.' Matthew 25:35-40

Holy Creator God, help us find your children, even in those that themselves in the lowest, meanest conditions for when you say **ALL**, we realize you truly mean ALL! Let us learn to Love our neighbors, brothers and sisters, and yes even our enemies for even the evil love their friends: You have heard that it was said, 'Love your neighbor and hate your enemy.' But I tell you, love your enemies and pray for those who persecute you, that you may be children of your Father in heaven. He causes his sun to rise on the evil and the good, and sends rain on the righteous and the unrighteous. If you love those who love you, what reward will you get? Are not even the tax collectors doing that? And if you greet only your own people, what are you doing more than others? Do not even pagans do that?

Matthew 5:43-48. Grant us peace and comfort as we continue to grow in your wisdom. We are so grateful for your patience and Love! We know that Gratitude is the doorway to a better world and a better life for all! AMEN

Day 85

A Devotional for Understanding and Acceptance

Where does our concept of fairness come from? What does it mean to be treated fairly? What does it mean to be treated unfairly? If we are to right a wrong done just 1 day ago, can we right that wrong without considering the impact the wrong made in the circumstances and conditions that exist now, just 24 hours after the wrong was committed? How about the impact after 1 week, a month, a year, a decade, or a century? What about the loss of resources that would have been advantageous for not just the individual wronged, but for all the heirs that were impacted by that loss for several generations?

When we consider the impact over time, and if that impact is spread to an entire class of people, we can begin to understand how various groups of people have either decided to say "forget it," and withdraw from the larger society, or even lash out at the power holders. How can Christians deal with these disparities based on what Christ taught us? Billy Graham, made this comment over 40 years: "Jesus was not a white man; He was not a black man. He came from that part of the world that touches Africa and Asia and Europe. Christianity is not a white man's religion, and don't let anybody ever tell you that it's white or black. Christ belongs to all people; He belongs to the whole world."

Jesus, being from the Middle East, was no stranger to the prejudice of trying to keep the lower classes down. As he said in Matthew 7:12 "So, whatever you wish that others would do to you, do also to them, for this is the Law and the Prophets." The Good News: This is literally "the golden rule" of the Bible. Do unto others as you would have them do unto you. In other words, if you want to be treated with kindness, be kind to others.

Glorious Creator God, hold us accountable but hold us in your heart. We know are not perfect yet we strive for a more perfect world. Too often we substitute our own notion of perfection for what we know is truly your ideal of perfection. In your perfect world, we would truly care about one another, not just with hollow words but with holy actions. We seek your guidance as we continue to make our ongoing efforts to reflect your love in all we do. Remind us every minute of every day, that achieving your Glory can only happen when our focus is on your commandments. When we realize that we must Love above all other actions, we will know we are on the right track. Yes, we do realize that we run the risk of losing our lives in many circumstances but help us remember your words dear Jesus: "For whoever wants to save their life will lose it, but whoever loses their life for me and for the gospel will save it" Mark 8:35

Day 86

A Devotional for Understanding and Acceptance

I was asked this morning, where did all this hate come from? And why did the Jewish people become the people hated most? As evidenced by accounting for 50% of all hate crimes in the US but making up less than 5% of the US population.

Hate violates every law of God. The 10 commandments are of 2 general types of basic laws. The first type relates to Loving God and second type is about Loving Our fellow humans, our neighbors, if you will. Every act of hate is a violation of the principles that underlie God's Laws and God's Creation. Some not so very Christian individuals twisted God's Laws and the Gospels to make them appear to suggest that "the Jews" were responsible for the Crucifixion of Jesus, but that is truly twisting the hateful actions of a few people that misinterpreted God's Laws and applying them to all people who were members of that same ethnic group. Jesus knew he was to die for the sins of mankind, and he accepted that as the necessary step to help heal mankind. His instructions to the Apostles and All followers of the faith was to share the Good News with all people. He told us that the message was not just for Jews but was to be shared with the entire world. He was not saying exclude the Jews, for goodness sake, Jesus was a Jew with a very long and notable genealogy of Jewish heritage.

Hating any person is a sin. Anyone who claims to be in the light but hates a brother or sister is still in the darkness.

Anyone who loves their brother and sister lives in the light, and there is nothing in them to make them stumble. 1 John 2: 9-10.

If someone says, "I love God," and hates his brother, he is a liar; for the one who does not love his brother whom he has seen, cannot love God whom he has not seen." 1 John: 4:20

In support of ☐ ending hate, very notably anti-Semitic hate, let's share our love for all people.

Gracious God, help us end "hate" and support the loving of all people. Please help all Christians accept the importance of our Jewish Brothers and Sisters in our own development as A Christian Faith. Please help us support the efforts to end Hate and the horrific crimes that hate generates! ☐ AMEN

Day 87

A Devotional for Understanding and Acceptance

We are fast approaching the most important season for all Christians, everywhere in our world. The Easter Season begins with the events leading up to the arrest, crucifixion, and resurrection of Jesus the Messiah. Tomorrow, Jesus, and his followers will make a fairly long journey from Jericho (an assumed location based on hints in the Gospels) to the House of Lazarus in Bethany. What happened in Jericho before the events in Bethany's and the triumphant entry of Jesus into Jerusalem?

There are many theories, but it is not explicitly stated. One of rt assumptions is that Jesus knew what was going to happen Tover the next several days, :so he was preparing himself t what was going to transpire. We know that just a few days before Jesus arrives at the house of Lazarus in Bethany, he received a message that Lazarus was very ill. But Jesus did not immediately leave for Bethany. When he arrives at Lazarus' house, he is informed that Lazarus had been dead for 4 days already.

On his arrival, Jesus found that Lazarus had already been in the tomb for four days. Now Bethany was less than two miles from Jerusalem, and many Jews had come to Martha and Mary to comfort them in the loss of their brother. When Martha heard that Jesus was coming, she went out to meet him, but Mary stayed at home. John 11: 17-20

"But, Lord," said Martha, the sister of the dead man, "by this time there is a bad odor, for he has been there four days."

Then Jesus said, "Did I not tell you that if you believe, you will see the glory of God?"

So they took away the stone. Then Jesus looked up and said, "Father, I thank you that you have heard me. I knew that you always hear me, but I said this for the benefit of the people standing here, that they may believe that you sent me." When he had said this, Jesus called in a loud voice, "Lazarus, come out!" The dead man came out, his hands and feet wrapped with strips of linen, and a cloth around his face. John 11: 39-44

Gracious God, Creator of All, this your season of promise. We are all filled with incredible hope and amazing gratitude based on the Amazing Grace you've shown us. As we progress through this Holy Easter Season help us remember that the awesome gift your Son has been to all of mankind, is a Gift of Joy and Love. Let there be no room for Hate and Harm in this Season or any Season. Grant us the Peace and Assurance of Salvation as we navigate this Easter Season. Let our hearts, minds, and intentions be open, loving, and full of your grace. Let us be true ambassadors of Christ in all that we do! AMEN!

Day 88

A Devotional for Understanding and Acceptance

In the days preceding the last supper, Jesus' arrest, his condemnation, trial, execution, burial, and his resurrection, Jesus continued to preach good news and predicted that these days would result in the temple being destroyed and in three days I will raise it up again. They thought he was talking about the Temple in Jerusalem, but he was referring to his body!

The Jews then responded to him, "What sign can you show us to prove your authority to do all this?" Jesus answered them, "Destroy this temple, and I will raise it again in three days." John 2:18-19

Jesus knew his role to be played out in the drama of human existence. The part of him that was human had real human thoughts and fears, just as you and I do. But, Jesus was also able to reach down inside himself to the place where, as the child of the living God, there was the indestructible seat of the eternal being that he wants us all to tap into.

Jesus answered him, "If anyone loves me, he will keep my word, and my Father will love him, and we will come to him and make our home with him. John 14:23

Whoever keeps his commandments abides in God, and God in him. And by this we know that he abides in us, by the Spirit whom he has given us. 1 John 3:24

Dwell in us oh Lord God of All Creation. Lead us to a union with your Holy Spirit within us as Jesus has taught us. There is no freedom or wealth or health without a union with your spirit. Let the sacrifice YOU made not be in vain. As we argue, fight, and work on ways to better deceive our neighbors, teach us all to value your creation more than our own Wealth, Ideas, Philosophies, and Possessions. Teach us to honor you by Loving our neighbor, for it is impossible to love you as fully as you deserve when we hate and deceive our neighbors. In this Easter Season, may we remember where our true allegiance lies! Either with this world or with you our Gracious Lord and Savior! AMEN

Day 89

A Devotional for Understanding and Acceptance

Why did Jesus give us the Parable of the Talents? What are we supposed to learn from that? Is it that the rich will always get richer, and the poor will always get poorer? I should say not! Let's look closer at this parable and we will see, it is a lesson about fear.

To one he gave five talents, to another two, to another one, to each according to **his ability.** Then he went away. Matthew 25:15

He also who had received the one talent came forward, saying, 'Master, I knew you to be a hard man, reaping where you did not sow, and gathering where you scattered no seed, **25** so I was **afraid,** and I went and hid your talent in the ground. Here, you have what is yours.' Matthew 25:24-25

God is calling on all of us to take what he has given us and make it grow. Do not hide your gift due to fear, lack of confidence, inadequate education, or for any other reason. At the time Jesus gave us these parables, he knew he was approaching his final days. In fact in just 3 days from now he will humble himself; imagine that the "KING OF KING AND LORD OF LORDS, "will ride into

Jerusalem on the back of a donkey, as humbly as he came into this world.

So many people are afraid they will look bad, not have enough money, not be smart enough, and/or lack poise. Forget all that! God does not care if you are afraid! He knows you will not likely face the same Fate as did Jesus. Boldly go where God asks you to God. Put fear behind you because giving into fear allows hate to replace love. Whatever creates paralyzing fear in our minds, blocks love from entering into our hearts. With love blocked, hatred takes over.

"Have I not commanded you? Be strong and courageous. Do not be afraid; do not be discouraged, for the Lord your God will be with you wherever you go." Joshua 1:9

Gracious God, our Creator, Redeemer, and Hope for the Ages, we know you've promised to be with us wherever we go yet fear still grips our hearts. We want to be champions for your cause. We want to be fully awake and aware of the gifts you've given us. Fear of what we do not know and do not understand causes us to bury the talent you've given us. Teach us to pray so that we can face our FEARS With the Courage it takes to truly be your Champions of A Loving Heart for ALL! This prayer is what has been given me as I've silently waited for what will give me what I need to do this!

Dear God and Jesus, my Savior! I am so grateful for the gifts you've given me. I'm so thankful for the love that you have given me and I have been blessed to receive from you all the time and energy I will ever need to share your love with others and the entire world. I know that I will receive from the world in proportion with what I give the world. And in the end, the love I receive will be determined by the love I freely give! Let me never be in need, for as long as I share all I have with love, I know I will always have all I need. AMEN

Day 90

A Devotional for Understanding and Acceptance

Today is the Friday Prior to Holy Week. Jesus had just spent the last 3 years traveling throughout the region, teaching, healing, and correcting the religious leaders of that era. He devoted his energy to working with ordinary people. God does not want us dependent upon legalistic religious leaders who felt that the only way to a truly great relationship with God was to follow all the laws and have the means to make the required sacrificial offerings in the temple. Jesus told us that was nonsense. He wanted us to follow what he felt were the two most important principles that would put us in alignment with God! Love God and Love you neighbor. He stated rather clearly that all the other laws can only be fulfilled if we make these two laws our focus and basis for all we do.

How are things different today? Unfortunately, legalistic people have forgotten the two most important laws. They'd rather point out what you are doing wrong than unconditionally love anyone. The Apostle Paul is also clear. In his 1st Letter to the Corinthians, chapter 13 verses 1-7, we are told what Paul thought about this Love Jesus tells us we need to show.

13 If I speak in the tongues of men or of angels, but do not have love, I am only a resounding gong or a clanging cymbal.**(Just a bunch of worthless noise)** If I have the gift of prophecy and can fathom all mysteries and all knowledge, and if I have a faith that can move mountains, but do not have love, I am nothing. **(Just parlor game or irrelevant tabloid newspaper)** If I give all I possess to the poor and give over my body to hardship that I may boast, but do not have love, I gain nothing. **(I'm an actor in a second-rate play)**

Love is patient, love is kind. It does not envy, it does not boast, it is not proud. It does not dishonor others, it is not self-seeking, it is not easily angered, it keeps no record of wrongs. Love does not delight in evil but rejoices with the truth. It always protects, always trusts, always hopes, always perseveres.

This Bible passage is read at so many weddings, I think it has lost its meaning for way too many people. For my family, these verses are the cornerstone of our family values. If large numbers of Churches ignore this, they just don't realize how harmful that is to the Christian Faith and the Truly Faithful followers of Christ.

Holy Creator God: teach us to love as you have loved. □ Help us remember that the first people you called to worship you were the Hebrew Nation. The people of Jewish heritage deserve our Love and Support as do all of Their lineage from Abraham, Jacob, the 12 Tribes, and the Nation of Israel. To you, however, national origin, race, the language we speak, the way that we approach you as our God, Creator, and Savior, is not as important as is our Love of You and all Your Creation. You've opened your salvation to all. For this we are truly Grateful! AMEN